REBUILDING YOUR LIFE WITH JESUS

TAYSHALEE REYES

DEDICATION

I first dedicate this book to the
Father, the Son, and the Holy Spirit.

My Aunt Kevelyn Laureano,
who was always a positive figure in my life leading to Christ.

I also honor my pastors, Christian and Nora Rivera,
through this book, for accepting me since day one,
for believing in me through my process,
and finally for sowing the seed of salvation in me.

INTRODUCTION

(Psalm 107:2-3 NIV)

"Let the redeemed of the Lord tell their story."

This book has been crafted with deep passion, commitment, and faith, aiming to resonate with those struggling with addiction, depression, and feelings of abandonment. It guides readers to discover Jesus as their liberator, savior, and healer: the embodiment of truth and the path to fulfillment. I firmly believe that sharing personal testimonies can break chains and liberate others.

Life encompasses more than what is visible; the struggles we face are genuine, yet it is through the Father, the Son, and the Holy Spirit that we can triumph and realize our true potential.

I invite you to explore my testimony and understand that God is indeed REAL.

TABLE OF CONTENTS

Chapter 1

Finding Your Way to Jesus

(Luke 15:20 NIV)

"So he got up and went to his father. But while he was still a long way off, his father saw him and was filled with compassion for him; he ran to his son, threw his arms around him and kissed him."

Oh Abba Father! I Praise you lord, I worship you with a grateful, joyful heart because you had rescue me from the hand of the enemy. Now I am no longer a slave of the enemy nor his instrument; now I am a CHILD of God being perfected day by day, I am His instrument and His precious vessel. I no longer must worry about tomorrow, because it is Him my life depends on. I no longer suffer anxiety because I refuge myself into his arms.

Philippians 4:6-7 (NIV) became one of my favorite practices in this beautiful path of finding Jesus: "Do not be anxious about anything, but in every situation, by prayer and petition, with thanksgiving, present your requests to God. And the peace of God, which transcends all understanding, will guard your hearts and your minds in Christ Jesus." What a wonderful verse, God promises us to protect our hearts and minds when we decide to rest and give up our burdens to Him. Throughout this walk of faith, I learned that Jesus is my best friend, my father, my husband, and my best companionship. When I'm facing fear or feeling weary, worried, sad, or anxious, He gives me the rest and the assurance that I need. The purpose in this chapter is for you to find rest in Jesus, while you are finding your way to Him. I invite you to rest in Him, leaving behind your stress, anxiety, sorrow, worries, problems, and all that troubles you and distracts you from finding Jesus. He wants you to enjoy the benefit of the peace that He offers you and to be able to rest in Him. I invite you at this moment to meditate on this verse, Matthew 11:28 (NIV), "Come to me, all you who are weary and burdened, and I will give you rest." That burden that you are carrying, that depression, those battling thoughts in your head, that pain in your heart, those concerns that consume your minds and heart every day do not belong to you; give them up to JESUS! Forming a relationship with God is having full dependency in Him, trusting Him, and having the faith that only He can change your story. Are you willing to give Jesus a try? Are you ready to walk with Jesus? Are you capable of letting Him in into your heart? Jesus is the healer, He is the restorer, the comforter that you need in your life.

He is the bread of life, He is the foundation that we need for us to function, because outside of Him there is nothing we can do. Jesus Himself said in John 15:5 (NIV), "I am the vine; you are the branches. If you remain in me and I in you, you will bear much fruit; apart from me you can do nothing." Jesus is life, the truth, and the way. He is calling you and waiting for you with open arms. He wants to hold you, to guide you, to instruct you to a path of wisdom, happiness, joy, and most importantly salvation. Before I started this wonderful path, I was broken and hopeless, I felt unloved, unheard, and lonely, I was battling with a low self-esteem, I had no direction, feeling lost, tired, and without purpose. Can you relate to any of these? Because if you do, you are NOT alone. In the book of Psalm 34:18 (NIV) it says, "The LORD is close to the brokenhearted and saves those who are crushed in spirit." God is right by your side; He listens to you and He will do what He has to do to rescue you!

I was attached to the spirits of depression, anxiety, suicidal thoughts, alcoholism, and fornication. All of the sudden my life changed when I was invited to church on the day of my birthday. You know, God is amazing. Sometimes He works in mysterious ways and, though we don't understand it, it ends up working well. For me to seek God, He had to remove things in my life that were not healthy. Before that best day happened in my life in which I accepted Jesus as my savior, I was in a long-term relationship. I found myself in love with and addicted to this relationship, though the way he treated me was not the best. I just had high hopes that one day he might change and love me. Yes! I spent too much time trying to make him love me. I was trying to fit into the world, but nothing worked. I was tired of using my own strength and resources to make him love me, to be noticed by him, and I finally concluded that the problem was me. Maybe I didn't belong in this world: maybe I am not pretty enough anymore, I am not smart, I am not special to anyone. All these thoughts started to govern my mind. For me to erase the pain in my heart, I sought refuge with drugs and alcohol. To make things worse, I left a great job for a terrible one. Yikes! When we don't have Jesus to guide us, we make foolish decisions because we let our hearts, thoughts, and the pleasure of the world guide us. The book of Proverbs is full of wisdom, and one of the verses that I can share pertaining to decision making is the following in Proverbs 14:12 (NIV), "There is a way that appears to be right, but in the end it leads to death."

The new job undoubtedly led to a detrimental lifestyle. It was situated in an environment filled with bars and clubs, which prompted me to consume alcohol daily. During my one-hour lunch break I would indulge in drinks, and after work I would accompany my colleagues to local bars for further enjoyment. I often disregarded the fact that I needed to return home to my beautiful toddler, who eagerly awaited my arrival. Life appeared enjoyable, characterized by socializing, drinking, and engaging with new colleagues. However, beneath my outward smile, I felt utterly lifeless. In my quest for love and solace, I sought refuge among the wrong people and wrong places. In my previous employment, I held a full-time position that included benefits such as health insurance and paid time off, with an hourly wage of $14.10, which was in the year 2019. I subsequently transitioned to a job that offered an hourly rate of $12.00, without any benefits, and limited to 35 hours per week. This decision proved to be quite detrimental, as my income significantly decreased. Compounding this situation, I also experienced a breakup with the father of my child due to issues of infidelity, which led me to relocate to an apartment with a rent of $800. While this amount may seem reasonable in 2024, it was quite burdensome for me as a single parent in 2019, struggling to make ends meet. Additionally, I found myself spending excessively on alcohol, dining out, and accumulating credit card debt.

My heart was shattered and I struggled to comprehend why it was so difficult for me to find a fulfilling relationship with someone who would love, respect, and remain loyal to me. The end of that relationship left me feeling increasingly isolated and I spent countless nights in tears. Those nights were cold and dark, filled with resentment, confusion, and repeated disappointments.

I often drifted off to sleep in a haze of alcohol, only to wake up disheartened and unmotivated to face the day ahead. My responsibilities as a mother took a backseat as I became consumed by my desire to escape my problems through drinking. Now, let's take a moment to reflect on this question: Have you ever felt as though the world was collapsing around you? Perhaps you felt abandoned by a higher power? If your answer is YES, then this book will only become more compelling!

I found myself without a partner, devoid of love and attention, grappling with my alcohol dependency. My new job had turned into a nightmare, filled with constant drama among coworkers, conflicts, and even instances of drug overdoses in the restroom. To make matters worse, I was facing sexual harassment from a supervisor. Yet, I feel trapped; leaving this job would jeopardize my ability to pay rent and provide for my child. Reflecting on my earlier thoughts about how God operates in mysterious ways, I realize that when He removes something from our lives, it is often to pave the way for new opportunities and to draw our focus back to Him. This became evident when, seemingly overnight, I began to feel increasingly uneasy and tense at work. Eventually, during a meeting, we were sent home early, and shortly after, I received a call from a secretary informing me that I was no longer employed.

Now, I found myself without a boyfriend, without love, and unemployed; factors that only worsened my desire to drink and deepened my depression. I felt utterly lost, with no job prospects and financial strain weighing heavily on me. It appeared that my life had come to a standstill, leaving me feeling vulnerable and questioning my will to live. One day, as I stared into the mirror, a voice echoed in my mind, telling me that no one loves me and that I should end my life. This led me to think of ways to finish with my life. I struggled to open up to others, primarily due to a lack of trust and the fear that no one would comprehend the battles I faced or the profound sorrow that consumed me. Each day, I found myself purchasing bottle after bottle of alcohol, feeling directionless and lost in those moments. One day, while browsing Facebook, I came across a video featuring a woman named Yesenia Then, who was sharing the message of God. The impact of that video was profound; it resonated deeply with me. I felt a renewed sense of hope, as if something was awakening within me. Following that moment, I began to watch her videos and sermons daily, which reignited my motivation and curiosity about Jesus. I started praying every day and listening to worship music, embracing this newfound spiritual journey.

Now I can understand Proverbs 4:22 (NIV), "For they are life to those who find them and health to one's whole body." The word of God is medicine to your soul, it has the power to heal you and to restore you. By hearing God's words through this preacher and by worshiping and praying I felt an impulse to keep going with life, that something big was coming my way. So, I tell you this my sisters and brothers SOMETHING BIG IS COMING YOUR WAY TOO! It has already begun! Do you believe it? It only takes a person to start believing again and that is called faith! I invite you to close your eyes and say with me, "I declare in Jesus name that something big is coming my way: changes, opportunities, life, hope, and restoration."

Reflecting on my past, I now realize that by choosing to listen to the word of God, engage in worship, and pray, I opened a new chapter in what was a challenging period of my life. The preacher I followed played a significant role in guiding me toward Jesus, Who illuminated my darkness. Jesus is the door we all need; He is the light and holds the answers to our struggles. I hope that my story inspires you to allow Jesus to brighten your life as well. As my birthday approached, I collaborated with my mother to organize a celebration with friends at a bar restaurant. She took the initiative to invite guests and purchase a cake. However, on the morning of November 10, 2019, my life took a turn with a simple text from my cousin Marc, who was attending church at the time. His invitation to join him at church resonated deeply within me, feeling like a divine call. Without hesitation, I agreed and called my mother to cancel the birthday plans. I remember her surprise as she asked, "Wait, you're going to church? Really? I've already invited friends." I firmly replied, "Please call them back and cancel; I need to go to church!"

(Isaiah 30:18 NIV)

"Yet the LORD longs to be gracious to you; therefore he will rise up to show you compassion. For the LORD is a God of justice. Blessed are all who wait for him!"

The moment had finally come! As I stepped into the church, an overwhelming sense of belonging washed over me. It felt inviting and safe, enveloping me in a profound peace that lifted all my burdens. It was as if God had been patiently waiting for my arrival. Throughout the service, tears flowed freely as I experienced the warmth and kindness of the pastors. When the pastor's wife approached me to pray, her words felt like a divine message from above. Her embrace was unlike any other; it was sincere and comforting, allowing me to lean on her as I cried, knowing it was God working through her. I felt an incredible sense of happiness, vitality, renewal, and joy in my heart. I had stepped into a new realm! I opened my heart to JESUS, my Savior. That day, I realized I had truly come home. I understood that He had been knocking on the door of my heart all along, always present for me, and that everything I had lost was part of my journey to seek Him and create space for a fresh start. Jesus is knocking at the door of your heart right now, longing to enter, to share moments with you, and to offer you peace, love, and guidance. Are you ready to open the door for JESUS?

(Revelation 3:20, NIV)

"Here I am! I stand at the door and knock. If anyone hears my voice and opens the door, I will come in and eat with that person, and they with me."

Chapter 2

JESUS IS LOVE AND RELATIONSHIP

(John 3:16 NIV)

"For God so loved the world that he gave his one and only Son, that whoever believes in him shall not perish but have eternal life."

Have you ever experienced love? It is a profound emotion that can inspire and motivate you in numerous ways. Whether it's love for your children, your family, your partner, or any aspect of life that evokes that deep sense of affection, love is truly a remarkable feeling. Love is everything. I will never forget March 3rd, 2015, the day I felt in love by first sight. My daughter Leenaysha was born and my heart melted. After that I wanted to try and leave behind the bad style of life I was living. I wanted to form a family, but something was missing. Though I had the love of my family, and I was so in love with my child, I needed something more than that; I felt incomplete. Do you feel like there is something missing in your life? You might have it all but still feel emptiness. When I met Jesus, I instantly knew that it was Him that I needed! The purpose of this chapter is for you to understand the love of Jesus for you.

One of the questions that I heard from unbelievers is, "What type of God would give His only Son to die on a cross for the world?" Well, a God that loves you, a God who just wants to have a communion and a relationship with His children, a communion that was lost when Adam and Eve disobeyed God by eating a fruit from the tree of knowledge of good and evil. Let me start from the beginning: When God created the world in Genesis between chapter 1-2, He saw that everything He created was good; that means He was happy with His own creation and it was meant for good, especially when He formed men and women. He said in the book of Genesis 1:26 (NIV), "Let us make man in our image, after our likeness." God created us similar to His image. He also provided for Adam and Eve in the garden of Eden; everything that was there belonged to them and they had dominion over everything except eating from the tree of knowledge of good and evil! Here I can say that they both had free choice to obey or disobey; God gives us free will to choose what path we want to take. Adam and Eve had a close, face-to-face relationship with God, but that changed when Adam and Eve disobeyed God. By eating from the tree of knowledge of good and evil their eyes were opened, they realized that they made the wrong decision and now they knew the bad and the good. They had opened a door of sin and spiritual death by just disobeying. After that, they were kicked out from the garden of Eden and they no longer had that close communion with God; now they had to work hard to supply for themselves. When reading the Old Testament, it is understandable that when Adam and Eve turned away from God, mankind was distorted and they became spiritually dead. All types of sin increased and they started to worship other false Gods, forgetting about God the creator and the covenant. This is what happens when we turn away from God, we are spiritually dead because the only one that can breathe life and bring light to our darkness is GOD.

The point I'm trying to make is that it was necessary for God to send His only Son because only He was holy, clean, and pure from sin. Jesus was the only way to save mankind. Now through Jesus we are saved when confessing that He is our only savior. The book of Romans 10:9 (NIV) says, "If you declare with your mouth, 'Jesus is Lord,' and believe in your heart that God raised him from the dead, you will be saved."

The best part of all is that His sacrifice was worthy for the comforter, the Holy Spirit, to come and abide in those that believe in Jesus as their savior. Through the Holy Spirit we can have a relationship, we can talk to God anywhere we go because the spirit abides in us, so that means that thanks to that sacrifice you are NOT ALONE, now you have a comforter who guides you, consoles you, and who walks with you. I recommend that you pause this moment and read the book of John chapter 16 in which Jesus is preparing His disciples for His departure and He speaks to them about the Holy Spirit.

Now that you have read chapter 16 of John, I want you do understand that God is NOT religion; He is love and relationship. After I accepted Jesus, I felt so much love. A type of love that made me felt like if I was floating in the air because I was finally able to rest, my sleepless nights were gone, I was sleeping like a baby having sweet dreams. I no longer had to worry about anything because the love I was feeling was so immense and supernatural that all I cared about was falling down on my knees and talking to God. I couldn't wait for Tuesdays' Bible class, I couldn't wait for Thursday nights and Sunday service! I wanted to always be in my heavenly father's business. Jesus is all about having a one-on-one relationship with Him, trusting in Him, humbling yourself before Him, depending on Him. The more you spend time with Jesus, the more you will look and act like Him. I started to love life, I started to see everything with a purpose, I even started to love those around me. Love and patience is a fruit that started to grow internally. In order for me to keep moving forward, the fruit of love was necessary; with love you can conquer anything starting with the kingdom of God! You might feel like you are losing if you don't receive someone's love back but that is a lie from Satan. 1 John 4:7-8 (NIV), says the following, "Dear friends, let us love one another, for love comes from God. Everyone who loves has been born of God and knows God. Whoever does not love does not know God, because God is love."

Hmm, let me guess. You might be thinking, "I have been heartbroken too many times, I can't open my heart to anyone, people have played with my feelings and I don't want to let anyone hurt me again." Yes, I understand exactly what it is to be broken and not trust anyone, but I am here to testify that God healed me and if He did it with me I believe He will do it with YOU. The Bible says in Psalm 147:3 (NIV), "He heals the brokenhearted and binds up their wounds."

When I decided to give Jesus a try, a lot of emotions were running through me. The times of betrayal by best friends who I dearly loved and trusted, rejections, lies, infidelities, and even betrayal in the family. In church I couldn't open up to anyone easily, I had put up walls around my heart and it wasn't easy for me to say hi, to be friendly, to interact with others, or to share problems or emotions. That was an area in my life that needed to be fixed and heal. Later on through the book we will talk about the healing process. However, due to being so hurt and broken, I realized that I was locking myself up into my own cell where no one had access and I was just hurting myself more. In order for God to work in us we need to open up and the best way is to pray about it, read His word, trust in Him. Building a relationship with the Holy Spirit is talking to Him about everything, your feelings, emotions, your fears, your gratitude, presenting to Him your daily tasks, your plans, just everything! And He will help you.

(1 Peter 5:6-7 NIV)

"Humble yourselves, therefore, under God's mighty hand, that he may lift you up in due time. Cast all your anxiety on him because he cares for you."

There is nothing that you are going through that Jesus can't fix. He cares so much for you that His graces, His love, His mercy, and His care wraps you up every day. Prayer and humbling are the keys to building a relationship with God, are the keys to your solutions, the keys to your healing and to a new beginning. Opening up with God is the beginning to your desires being fulfilled, the beginning of joy and peace to your life, and healing to your soul. I have heard people tell me, "I do not know how to pray," and that is a common statement of many, but let me explain that prayer is communication with a loyal, open heart believing and not doubting. When I am not sure what to say, I start to praise how good and faithful He is. I begin my prayers with thanksgiving and acknowledge everything He has done. I worship in my room for two to three songs to connect and glorify Him and then I kneel to pray along with the Bible because God is amazing in speaking to you through His words. Below I will leave two verses for you to meditate on about prayers.

*"Therefore, I tell you, whatever you ask for in prayer,
believe that you have received it, and it will be yours."*

In other words, believe what you are praying for and it will
be given to you!

(Romans 8:26 NIV)

*"In the same way, the Spirit helps us in our weakness.
We do not know what we ought to pray for, but the
Spirit himself intercedes for us through wordless
groans."*

The enemy is always going to try to make you fall, to stop
you from praising and take you out of communion with God,
because he knows that you can't function without God. Eve was
deceived by Satan, that is how she was tempted to eat from the
tree of knowledge. So it is important to remain focused, always
praying diligently, even when times are hard and you may be
discouraged; do NOT stop praying!

God loves us so much and there is no love, no grace, no
mercy, and no faithfulness compared to His. I believe that if
you truly set in your minds and hearts that Jesus loves you and
cares for you, your perspective about life, yourself, and others will
change. You no longer must try to fit in with a crowd of friends,
you don't have to depend on pleasing or winning other people's
love, because God loved you first. If you have already opened
your door to Jesus, now is the time to deepen your relationship
with Him. Understanding that He gave Himself at the cross for

LOVE, so that that through Him we can rest. The death of Jesus on the cross tore the veil that separated us from direct access to His presence, granting us full access to establish a relationship with Him. Through Him, you can experience salvation and forgiveness and discover the true love you have been searching for. Begin your meditation now; close your eyes and pray to your Savior.

Heavenly Father, I express my gratitude for the sacrifice you made for me on the Cross. Thank you for loving me even when I was still a sinner. I pray that from this day forward, my relationship with you will deepen. Please guide me in my daily prayers, reveal your ways to me, and help me resist temptation. Be my refuge in times of weakness and fatigue and be my light in moments of darkness. Assist me in living a life that pleases and honors you. Amen.

Chapter 3

GOD IS OUR PROVIDER

(Philippians 4:19, NIV)

"And my God will meet all your needs according to the riches of his glory in Christ Jesus."

Establishing a relationship with God involves relying on Him and recognizing that He will meet our needs in every aspect of our lives. God is aware of our deficiencies, our requirements, and our innermost aspirations. In the first chapter, I shared my experience of being unemployed, which made it challenging to manage my rent and bills with the limited income I received from unemployment benefits. However, during this difficult period, God instilled in me a sense of peace and assurance. I had faith that He would somehow meet my needs. During church services, when it was time to worship through offerings and tithes, I would contribute the little I had remaining. When you offer God everything you possess, no matter how small, and place your trust in Him, it brings Him joy and opens the door for His blessings.

The story of the widow's offering in the temple helped me understand that when we give it all to Christ, He takes care of us.

God sees everything; He sees your despair, He sees your heart and your needs. The book of Mark 12:43-44 (NIV) says, "Calling his disciples to him, Jesus said, 'Truly I tell you, this poor widow has put more into the treasury than all the others. They all gave out of their wealth; but she, out of her poverty, put in everything—all she had to live on.'"

God is looking for individuals who are willing to dedicate themselves fully and worship Him sincerely, even when they feel they have nothing left to offer. Like the widow, your heart and faith are sufficient for Him. The widow contributed everything she possessed with genuine faith and integrity, disregarding the judgments of others regarding her offering, as she trusted that her heavenly Father would provide for her needs. While those around us may critique our expressions of worship, I have come to understand that our actions should be aimed at pleasing God rather than seeking the approval of others.

One time I found myself in a difficult situation regarding the rent, as I was short by $200.00 with only a week remaining. In hopes of a miracle, I gathered the money I had stored in a tote bag hanging in my closet. A few days later, the father of my child provided me with the necessary funds to cover the rent. When I returned to the closet to secure the money he had given me, I began counting the amount I had previously set aside, and to my astonishment, I discovered that I had more than I initially thought! Before adding the funds from my child's father, I realized that I already possessed the full rent amount in the tote bag. Overwhelmed with joy, I wept with excitement, recognizing that it was a divine intervention during my time of need. I was even able to keep the extra money for myself! In moments of despair, remember that divine assistance is at work. Do you believe in this?

It was that time of year: Christmas was just around the corner, and I still didn't have a tree because I couldn't afford one.

One morning, I decided to check my bank account to see if my unemployment deposit had come through, and to my surprise, I found I had more money than I expected. I tried to figure it out, but it just didn't add up. It felt like a miracle, like God was multiplying what little I had. Feeling incredibly blessed, I dashed to the store to grab a tree and some decorations. When the cashier scanned my items, I was shocked to see the prices drop. She kept trying to scan them again, probably thinking something was off, but I just laughed and said, "Stop trying; God's blessings are upon me!" She chuckled, and I ended up getting a Christmas tree and decorations for a great price. That same day, I had invited my pastors and a few friends from church over, and I had planned to make one pan of lasagna. Thanks to the unexpected money, I was able to whip up two pans instead!

The reason why I'm sharing this testimony of God's provision is for you to understand that if we place God first above all, He will not forsake us. Let's read the book of Hebrew 13:5 (NIV), "Keep your lives free from the love of money and be content with what you have, because God has said, 'Never will I leave you; never will I forsake you.'"

Look beyond the material world and focus on the higher things, and you'll notice God's blessings not just in your finances, but also in your heart and spirit. I pray in Jesus' name that you, the reader of this book, will experience the Holy Father's provision in your life, that He showers you with blessings and fills your heart with peace even when times are tough. Always remember, He's by your side and will never abandon you. Jesus isn't just about meeting your physical needs; He's also here to nourish your spirit. If you're feeling spiritually parched, He's ready to quench your thirst, and if you're craving a deeper connection with Him, He'll feed that hunger.

Embracing Jesus represents a significant transformation in our lives, marking a profound change. It is important to acknowledge that this journey is not without its challenges. We may experience feelings of discouragement and fear, and at times, we might contemplate giving up. However, God consistently finds ways to support us during our moments of despair. Engaging with Him daily through prayer, worship, and participation in church services serves as a means for spiritual nourishment. The more diligently we seek Him, the more we will discover His presence. Are you familiar with the account of how God utilized Moses to liberate the Israelites from their bondage in Egypt? If not, I encourage you to pause and explore the book of Exodus, particularly chapters 16.

The Israelites were going through a big change, moving from slavery to freedom while relying on God in the desert. They felt scared, hungry, and down, and eventually, they vented to Moses in Exodus 16:3 (NIV) saying, "If only we had died by the LORD's hand in Egypt! There we sat around pots of meat and ate all the food we wanted, but you have brought us out into this desert to starve this entire assembly to death."

It's totally normal to feel down and scared at this moment, especially when you think back to how things were before you found Jesus. But remember, God is right there with you, even in your toughest times, like when you're feeling lost in that desert of doubt and fear. Sometimes, He leads us into those dry places so we can really see that He's in control and that He's the one who brings us what we need from above.

I'm not sure what kind of desert you're wandering through right now or what you might need. But I do know that Jesus is the way. Just like He saw the widow's heart when she gave from her poverty, He sees yours too. He provided for the Israelites in the desert, and He'll do the same for you. Just keep God as your top priority!

"But seek first his kingdom and his righteousness, and all these things will be given to you as well."

Chapter 4

Rebuilding the Walls of Your Heart

(Nehemiah 2:2 NIV)

"So the king asked me, 'Why does your face look so sad when you are not ill? This can be nothing but sadness of heart.'"

Alright! You've made it to chapter four. The past few days might have been tough for you. Right now, you could be dealing with feelings of sadness, grief, or a broken heart. You might be anxious about how things will turn out. As you read this chapter, you might be hoping for a message from God. Just like the king recognized Nehemiah's pain, God is watching you right now and sees what's in your heart. So get ready! In this chapter and beyond, we're going to explore the word, share my story, and connect with your heart. It's time for some healing and restoration!

Your heart is the altar of God, the protection of your heart is important in our everyday life. The book of Proverbs 4:23 (NIV) says, "Above all else, guard your heart, for everything you do flows from it." What we hold in our heart is what reflects in our outer self. When someone hurts you, it is mainly because in their heart they are bitter and broken. Do not blame yourself anymore for the past or how people treated you, their way of treating you was the reflection of what they carry in their heart. Painful experiences, betrayals, hardships, disappointments, deceptions, grudges, lack of forgiveness, and feelings of hate burn down the walls of our heart.

I began attending church regularly on Tuesdays, Thursdays, and Sundays, and I really loved being around everyone. The warmth from my amazing pastors, leaders, and God made everything feel so beautiful. However, deep down, I was still hurting. I had old wounds and painful memories that I just couldn't shake off. When you embark on a journey of faith, the enemy will always try to drag your past back into your mind, making you feel unworthy of God's forgiveness and healing. He doesn't want you to heal because He knows that once you do, and you rebuild the walls of your heart, you'll start to see God's purpose for you and become a powerful tool in His hands.

Nehemiah chapter 4 dives into the story of Nehemiah as he kicks off the rebuilding of Jerusalem's wall. During this time, he faced opposition from enemies who plotted against him to disrupt the work. But here's the thing: being broken doesn't mean you can't be used by God. When you're on the path of God's purpose, the enemy will do everything he can to throw you off and cause you pain again and again!

I couldn't let go of the memories of infidelities, asking myself every day, "What did I do to deserve this?" I also couldn't let go of the betrayals of my best friends; I felt like the more I loved someone the more I would be broken, so I asked myself, "how can I love again?" Years ago, before giving my life to Christ, I decided on an abortion. It was one of my most painful decisions and experiences. I always lived with guilt and wished to go back and undo it. I thought I would never forgive myself for it and the enemy (Satan) knew those guilts that I carried, so it was a great way to torment me. I always asked God, "Will I meet my aborted child one day and ask for forgiveness"? I had feelings of guilt and grief. I dreamed of babies every night, the enemy reminded me every day of the hopeless, broken, drunkard women that I was. However I understood that the same way Satan tries to break you with your past, God uses the broken part of you to glorify Himself; He uses your pain to wake up a new version of you.

Words can't explain the hurt and the brokenness in me, and though I was in church I was still in the process of restoring my soul. The Lord knew the pain and the memories of the past that I was carrying, and it was up to me to allow Him to restore me. But I decided to do like this man Nehemiah; I was not going to sit back and let the enemy keep playing with my mind, reminding me and accusing me about the past. Nehemiah was not going to allow the walls to remain destroyed, he was not going to allow the enemies to go in and out and do with Jerusalem as they pleased. Nehemiah did not let his pain, sadness, and bad news stop him! Instead he fasted and prayed day and night to the lord of heavens, but the part that I loved the most is when he reminds God of His promise to Moses in the book of Nehemiah chapter 1:8-9.

I decided not to let my past and pain dictate my life anymore. Instead, I chose to focus on the promises God has made to me. I reflected on His words and how He has redeemed and forgiven me. I realized I'm a new creation in Him, wonderfully made. I prayed for the Lord to refresh my mind, thoughts, heart, and soul. I began to allow God to heal my wounds by believing in His promises and putting my trust in Him. I came to understand that God has a purpose for me, and He has one for you too! Your broken heart has a purpose in His plan! What once hurt me has now turned me into a stronger, more powerful tool in God's hands.

God allows us to go through certain painful experiences, even if it is betrayal, separation, sickness, rape, addiction, abusive relationships, a dysfunctional family, a loss of someone, and much more that can mark us forever, because He knows that one day we will become a powerful testimony that will break the chains and bondage of others, that will reach to ears of people in need of hope. Just like Nehemiah, He will transform you into a great leader to help restore other broken walls.

In this life there will always be afflictions, hardships, disappointment but as long as Jesus is within you, there is nothing to fear. Read the following verse in John 16:33 (NIV): "I have told you these things, so that in me you may have peace. In this world you will have trouble. But take heart! I have overcome the world."

So get up today! Do not be a victim anymore and let God help you restore the walls of your heart. Jesus overcame the world, if He is with you nothing can stop you, you can also overcome the afflictions of this world. I invite you to pray more, separate time for God, be sincere to Him and present to Him how you feel. Write down all the promises of God in your life and what He has done in you. Speak the name of Jesus over your pain, over your past, and remind yourself that you are chosen for greater things. Nehemiah was able to conquer by following what God placed in his heart, to rebuild the burning walls, so now is your time to conquer what God has for you! And remember there is nothing that can separate you from the love of God; it doesn't matter how despicable your past was, what sins you had committed, how many people may rise against you, what people may think or say of you, it will not succeed from separating you from God. Just like Sanballat, Tobiah, and Arabs tried to rise against Nehemiah, they were unable to stop him from doing God's will because if God is with you who is against you?

So today I rebuke in Jesus' name every spirit of Tobiah and Sanballat that want to stop you from walking in God's purpose, I rebuke in Jesus' name the lies of the enemy that says you are not worthy of God's love and healing, because you were redeemed with the blood of the lamb. I rebuke in Jesus' name those battling thoughts and pain in your heart that doesn't allow you to open your heart and form a relationship with others. I declare in Jesus' name that the walls of your heart will be restored and God will prepared a strong leader in you to conquer lives for Jesus and to be able to walk in his promise. Amen !

Here's a verse for you to reflect on and use as a shield against anything that tries to keep you from rebuilding the walls of your heart:

(Roman 8:37-39 NIV)

"No, in all these things we are more than conquerors through him who loved us. For I am convinced that neither death nor life, neither angels nor demons, neither the present nor the future, nor any powers, neither height nor depth, nor anything else in all creation, will be able to separate us from the love of God that is in Christ Jesus our Lord."

Chapter 5

Don't Look Back

(Genesis 19:26 NIV)

"But Lot's wife looked back, and she became a pillar of salt."

Church was wonderful; I felt a part of me healing. I became more friendly, opened up to others, and changed how I dressed, acted, and spoke. Unfortunately, I was still struggling with worldly pleasures. I couldn't stop drinking. I asked God, "How can I quit when I've been drinking since I was twelve?" I felt unworthy of His love and guilty for attending church while still drinking. It seemed impossible to give it up, and I was scared. I knew I needed to let go of many things, but I didn't know how. I thought life would be dull without wine or margaritas.

The narrative of Lot and his wife in Genesis 19 serves as a poignant reminder of the necessity to move forward and not dwell on the past once one has been liberated by God. The cities of Sodom and Gomorrah were steeped in wickedness, their transgressions significant in the eyes of the Lord. Lot, along with his wife and children, resided in these cities, and the scripture recounts that God dispatched two angels to alert Lot of the impending destruction. Let us pause for a moment. Can you reflect on the instances when God has sent someone to assist you, to caution you, or to convey His message through another? Often, we overlook these opportunities as we become preoccupied with our own desires, neglecting the divine intention to offer us a renewed life. I recall a particular church anniversary when I felt spiritually drained, on the verge of surrendering. That day, I contemplated not returning to church, overwhelmed by my inability to overcome my drinking habits. I found myself in a constant struggle about attending services, gradually losing hope. Many of us have experienced similar feelings of despair, contemplating giving up due to a lack of willpower to forsake worldly pleasures. Whether it be an addiction to substances, harmful friendships, toxic relationships, or any other distractions that divert our focus from God, it can feel like an unending spiritual conflict. I distinctly felt as though my spirit was in a constant struggle. After the service concluded, the pastor's mother approached me and said, "If you stray from this path, it will lead you to death." Those words struck me deeply, though I did not fully grasp their meaning at the time; it was undoubtedly a warning. Much like the angels sent to Lot, God provided me with a crucial message. Returning to Lot's story, as they fled the city, God commanded them not to look back. However, Lot's wife turned to gaze back, her heart still tethered to the pleasures of her former life in that city. She was so accustomed to her old life that she wasn't ready to embrace a fresh start. By focusing on the past, she became like a statue of salt, which is a fate many of us face. When God offers us a chance to break free from sin, our hearts often cling to old habits, addictions, and worldly pleasures. By looking back, we miss out on the new life God wants to provide, hindering our spiritual growth and leaving us trapped in a cycle of trying to fix things on our own.

I want you, right at this moment, to stop and meditate on this questions: What are the barriers that prevent you from growing spiritually? Are you willing to renounce them today? Will you be like Lot who was obedient and kept his eyes forward, or will you look back like his wife?

Looking back can hold us back from fulfilling God's purpose in our lives. The Israelites spent forty years wandering in the desert because their hearts and minds were still tied to Egypt. I struggled to grow spiritually, losing my joy and happiness, which led to bitterness. Loneliness crept in, making my nights feel long and cold again. I became disheartened with the church, and feeling isolated, I decided to reconnect with my child's father. I went back to something God had already freed me from. I tried to handle things on my own, not realizing I was heading toward spiritual death. I wanted to do things my way and became rebellious. I attended church three times a week but continued drinking and fornicating. I didn't allow God into my heart; even in church, I felt distant. Gradually, I was fading away. I felt like a hypocrite, full of sin and anger, and I began to drift away from everyone. Now, I understand the words of the pastor's mother. I was living in death, just as the book of James 1:15 (NIV) warns, "Then, after desire has conceived, it gives birth to sin; and sin, when it is full-grown, gives birth to death."

Ouch! sounds bad, doesn't it? I felt worse than bad, I felt like the worst human being in the world. Then the voices in my head started: "Why are you still going to church? You are not worthy, you are a hypocrite and a sinner, you will never be free, no one will forgive you. Look at you! You are nobody! You can't do it. You are weak! No one loves you! Do not dare to worship. God won't receive your praise." The voices of condemnation were governing me day and night and I started to believe them. I became angry with everyone, my heart felt dark and bitter, I started to think that

God had forsaken me, so I started to blame Him for everything. I even started to feel jealous of seeing others' marriages restored, others growing spiritually and others getting married while I was there battling, sad and deep in sorrow. I blamed everyone. I felt like no one cared. The enemy blinded me and took over my mind and heart. I was already planning to leave the church. I stopped listening to worship music, I stopped listening to sermons, and I became totally enraged. Months passed, my relationship with my spouse wasn't working. I tried so hard to make him happy, to please him, I tried so hard to be happy with him and to feel loved by him, but jealousy, lies, arguments, obsession, anxiety, and depression were taking over me. The relationship was worse than before. I lost control and I began to drink more heavily, but this time, due to my depression, I was mixing in sleeping pills as well to numb my pain. I felt far away from God; I literally saw myself surrounded by darkness. I felt my heart bleeding, and my soul perishing more and more. I lost the desire for everything until one day the thoughts of ending my life entered my head again. I did not want to live anymore; I wanted to end this for once! But there was something in me, there was something left in me, I felt it, there was a little spark of fire left within me. I couldn't run away from church, the more I thought about it, even if I had to come in with a hangover I just couldn't stay home. I felt a fire that urged me to go. Church was my only hope, even if I was not willing to worship, praise, or open my heart. There was something alive inside of me that prevented me from fleeing. I related so much with Jeremiah; he no longer wanted to speak about God, he wanted to give up, but the word of God burned in him like fire. Though I was afflicted, I knew that I couldn't just run away from Him, from His words and promise. The fire of God kept pulling be back, is what kept me holding and going. God was so deep in me! Yes, and that fire is deep in you too, the more you try to run away from God, He is right there by your side. If you have been feeling tired from battling in this walk of faith, I want to declare right now in the powerful name of Jesus that the fire that is within you will burn so deep into your bones and consume you until you surrender at Jesus' feet. Do not give yourself up to the world! Surrender it all to Jesus!

In this difficult part of my life, I was so grateful to know that I was not alone. Besides God, I had my pastors who I know prayed so much for me. My pastor's wife never gave up on me! She was attentive to me and there were times when she would pull me to the office to guide me. One time I was running late to church, and I remember seeing a text message from her asking me if I was coming to church, and then to a few seconds later she told me, "I am not giving up on you that easily." How beautiful it was to know that though I was giving up on myself, there was someone who believed in me and was not willing to let me go. Why am I sharing this? Because when you find yourself in a hard time, it is important to value and honor those leaders, pastors, and friends that God places in your life to help you and guide you.

I was still here, trying too hard to make my emotional relationship succeed. Even though he once said he didn't want to marry and wouldn't change, I just couldn't bring myself to let him go. I found myself drawn to his presence, craving the comfort of companionship, yet my heart remained unfulfilled. During our intimate moments, I experienced an even deeper sense of emptiness. A nagging feeling told me that my actions were misguided. While I had always viewed fornication as a natural expression of love, this time felt distinct. I had come to understand that sex is intended for marriage and engaging in it outside of that commitment felt like a transgression of the spirit. I came to the realization that I was not appreciating my own worth, and embracing my identity as a new creation meant dedicating myself to God. One evening, after a particularly intense argument, he uttered something so hurtful that it sparked a profound awakening within me. I understood that he would never change, regardless of my efforts, and I could no longer continue living in this manner. Standing in the kitchen, I felt a mix of confusion and clarity. I remained silent, trying to process everything swirling in my mind. A voice within me whispered, "You deserve better; you are valuable." I want to take this opportunity to remind you that you are indeed valuable, a reflection of God's perfection, and you are deeply loved. Those who have caused you pain were unable to recognize your unique worth, but one day, those who abandoned you, hurt you, betrayed you, or doubted you will witness the transformed version of you in God's embrace.

A week went by without any calls or messages from my partner, prompting me to engage in meditation and reflect on my situation. My depression deepened as I began to grapple with feelings of regret, sorrow, and isolation simultaneously. While I was in my room, overwhelmed by a whirlwind of emotions and thoughts, a verse from Isaiah suddenly resonated with me.

(Isaiah 55:8-9 NIV)

> "'For my thoughts are not your thoughts, neither are your ways my ways,' declares the LORD.
> 'As the heavens are higher than the earth, so are my ways higher than your ways and my thoughts than your thoughts.'"

My ways are not God's ways, my plans are not God's plans, my thoughts are not God's thoughts. My strength was not enough. I needed something bigger, almighty, powerful, and higher than me. I needed a divine intervention from God. I was chained up with darkness and death surrounding me. Everything was making sense. Satan was trying to pull me out of church, he had me blinded with grudge, bitterness, and addiction. It was nobody's fault but mine! I left my Father's home, but now it was time for me to come back. I remember telling myself, "How did I end up like this again? What have I done?" I was better off at my Father's house, though I had battles, it was better to go through it in His presence! I fell down on my knees, I cried out to God, I finally opened my mouth and started to worship. The atmosphere shifted from darkness to light and peace, the weight on me was lifted. I shouted "Satan, you can't have me no more, I am a daughter of God and He is not done with me." My mouth was shut for a long time, but once I started to praise and cast out what was tormenting me there was a relief in my soul. I felt the presence of God surrounding my room after such a long time. I cried and confessed to Him my mistake and how sorry I was.

This is the time! The time for you to open your mouth and worship. Use your worship like a weapon against the spirits that are torturing you. Allow your worship to God to be bigger than your problems. God is not done with you! He is still working in you, He is still by your side. So open your mouth, Hallelujah and worship the most high, because He is your freedom! When you don't feel the desire to worship, that is when you have to worship and praise harder! Pray harder! Cry out higher until the doors of heaven are opened to you! Let your cry reach the throne of God and He will incline His ears to you. Because He is not done with you! Just like the book of Philippians 1:6 (NIV) says, "being confident of this, that he who began a good work in you will carry it on to completion until the day of Christ Jesus."

Before God, I humbled myself and pleaded for His presence to renew my spirit and restore my first love. Overwhelmed with emotion, I expressed my feelings of being lost and directionless, asking for His guidance to illuminate my path. As I knelt in tears, a voice within me resonated, urging me to make a choice: would I continue to dwell in the world or choose to walk in the light?

(Deuteronomy 30:15 NLT)

"Now listen! Today I am giving you a choice between life and death, between prosperity and disaster. For I command you this day to love the LORD your God and to keep his commands, decrees, and regulations by walking in his ways. If you do this, you will live and multiply, and the LORD your God will bless you and the land you are about to enter and occupy."

There was a decision to be made between the world and the light.

Chapter 6

GET RID OF IT!

(2 Corinthians 5:17 NIV)

"This means that anyone who belongs to Christ has become a new person. The old life is gone; a new life has begun!"

In Christ, we are no longer the same person meaning that we no longer practice what we used to do without Christ. God sees us differently; He sees us holy and redeemed through the holy, pure blood of His Son that cleansed us. When we encounter God, something needs to break; the atmosphere in our lives shifts and our minds must renovate because we are children of God. We should no longer walk in darkness but in light. Jesus himself said in John 5:25 (NIV), "Very truly I tell you, a time is coming and has now come when the dead will hear the voice of the Son of God and those who hear will live." Though this word is in regards to the resurrection, it also applies to the present. The spiritually dead can hear God's Word and when they truly accept it in their hearts, the barriers the devil has created are removed. Those who were lost in sin can now find eternal life through Jesus, becoming new beings and letting go of their past by believing that Jesus died for their sins. We must abandon our old habits and behaviors that keep us from living in the light. Jesus' light should shine through us, but it can be challenging. This is where my testimony comes in, as I leave my past behind, reject sin, and take up my own cross.

(Luke 14:27 NIV)

"And whoever does not carry their cross and follow me cannot be my disciple."

You might be asking, "What does carrying my own cross mean?" Well, it means denying yourselves and submitting completely to God's perfect will. Jesus carried our sin to the cross; that was the Father's will. He suffered humiliation, shame, betrayal from His own people, torture, and much more. Now it was my time to live for Jesus. Chapter five ended with me having to decide: choose between light or the darkness. I got so tired of battling on my own and of living a life full of darkness. In that moment, when that voice spoke inside of me telling me to make a decision, my eyes were opened. I knew I was in spiritual warfare and I had to submit myself completely to God because I couldn't fight it alone and God was calling out to me. It was like being in a dark deep pit but also seeing God's hands reaching out to me from above. He was there! Calling me!

YOU! Yes, God is calling out to you! He is waiting for you; His mercy and love endure forever, but He also wants to open your eyes. Those battles in your life do not belong to you; stop fighting alone and let Jesus in! You are free only if you allow yourself to be free by believing in faith and trusting God in those deep areas in you that you are not willing to give up. That internal pain, that hidden feeling or sin that you are holding on to, it is time to let it out in Jesus' name and regain the life that Jesus has given you through His death on the cross. He is telling you, "Get up and carry your cross," but the best part is that you won't have to carry it alone because He is right by your side.

On that night of spiritual awakening, I decided to follow Christ. There were two main areas in my life that were holding me back: the unhealthy relationship I had with the father of my child and the drug abuse with alcohol. I said to myself, "First things first," so I grabbed my phone and searched in my contacts for my spouse's name. When I think of this scenario in my life, it becomes so vivid in my mind because it was a painful decision. I was about to leave behind the love of my life: the thing that I fought most for. It was time to let it go. With tears rolling down my cheeks, I texted him, saying "I am going to follow Jesus," and he responded with a question, "Are you leaving me?" And crying my eyes out, I responded, "Yes." After that, he did not respond, beg, or say anything, and that is how I understood that it was God's will. God loved me too much to see me suffer in a relationship that was painful; He had to remove me out of that relationship to start His perfect work in me. When God removes you from a place, a job, or people it is because He wants to start a work in you that can only happen with Him and you, and with nothing else that gets in the way. He wants your full heart and attention.

I admire how Jesus' disciples gave up everything to follow Him. They realized that just believing wasn't enough; being a disciple meant walking with Jesus through both good and bad times. This brought them closer to Him, allowing them to learn more and become like Him. Imagine those days without cars or buses, just miles of walking behind a man who claimed to be the

Son of God. He brought hope, light, guidance, and purpose into their lives. I felt it was my time to not only believe but also to become a disciple, leaving my past behind, even if it meant facing suffering and sacrifice. It was worth it because I no longer had to rely on falsehoods. Yet, my heart ached, especially at night when I missed my ex-boyfriend deeply. The hardest part was our lack of contact, and my daughter would cry at night, missing her dad. Her questions of, "Why can't I see Dad? Why isn't he coming anymore?" broke my heart. The shared pain between my daughter and me was overwhelming. I had to numb the pain again, so I kept drinking. I would pick up the glass of wine with sadness knowing that it wasn't the right thing to do, but I didn't have the willpower to stop. Again, drowning myself into the pain and feeling of grief.

In each service, I would pray to God, asking Him to speak to me and help me quit drinking. I needed guidance on how to stop something I had done for so long. My body craved alcohol all the time; I relied on it to get through the day. One day, while kneeling at the altar, I said, "God, I left my daughter's father for you and stopped fornicating. How can I let go of alcohol now?" Days passed and I was still waiting for God to show me and talk to me, my spirit longed for God's voice. All I wanted was for Him to tell me, "Stop," but I knew that He was teaching me how to be patient. God is really patient with us, and that is the same way He wants us to be. When God remained silent I learned that is because He is working and we just need to be patient.

PRAY AND BE PATIENT

(Romans 12:12 NIV)

"Be joyful in hope, patient in affliction, faithful in prayer."

So I started to pray against my addiction, with all my heart I prayed that God would help me to have the will power to stop drinking, that He might give me the strength from above, that He would take away my fleshly desires. I told God that I didn't want to be the same anymore, I wanted to be a different person, I wanted to walk differently. I prayed day and night nonstop, because the addiction was the biggest yoke I was battling with. I needed His anointing to break this yoke.

One time I was in the kitchen pouring myself some wine to watch a movie and I remembered asking myself in a reflective way, "Do I really need this cup of wine?" but I just ignored myself and sat on the couch. When I took a sip it tasted so horrible, almost like medicine and I looked at it and smelled it thinking that maybe it was rotten but again I ignored it and kept drinking it. No matters how bad it tasted; I came to a conclusion that it was already a habit of mine to drink. Every bottle of wine and margarita I was buying started to taste so differently, I was making strange faces while drinking it because I suddenly couldn't figure out why it tasted so bad.

Let me pause right here! Because there is something that has to be cleared up. People say that it is not a sin to drink as long as you don't get drunk. From my experience drinking alcohol was making me feel emptier because I was placing alcohol before God as a refuge and that is a sin. God doesn't want us to sit in sorrow and waste our life drinking, He wants us to have a conscious, clear mind to make decisions, to function. He wants us to be wise and fruitful, not to be lazy. Drinking everyday was like fog in my brain, I couldn't think clearly, I couldn't work the next day, I wanted to sleep, I was always tired, I felt vulnerable, lonelier and emptier. Read the following verses in regards to drinking: Proverbs 23:29-30, Proverbs 23:33. Addiction to alcohol is having no self-control, and not having self-control leads to poor choices (Proverbs 23:12–25). But I love this verse in Ephesians 5:18 (NIV), which says, "Do not get drunk on wine, for that is debauchery. Instead be filled with the Spirit." Alcohol or any type of drug is not the way or the solution to your problems, but being filled by the spirit of God allows us to walk in wisdom, joy, and confidence. We are the temple of the Holy Spirit, for the spirit to dwell in us we need to separate ourselves from things that lead us astray. Wine or any type of drugs and alcohol has the power to enslave us if we let it. And I wanted to break that! I was ready to break my generational curse! What are the generational curses that need to be broken in your family?

Back to my story, indeed I was getting frustrated, though alcohol did not taste the same anymore I couldn't help it but to continue drinking. I kept praying but I was running out of patience asking God where He was. This is when I wanted God to step in already, otherwise I was already thinking to place myself in rehab. No response from God, no signs, and I was going mad. Can you relate to this? wanting God to do something, but nothing happens? Crying out to Him for days and night but no response? Are you seeking for Gods answer in regards to something? I have news for you! God's timing is perfect, He hasn't forgotten you, He is still working! Whatever situation you are trying to get out of, God has the way and the time. The same God that divided the sea for the Israelites to be free is the same God that will also open a path for you! Keep being patient and do not dismay! The Bible says in James 1:3 (NKJV), "knowing that the testing of your faith produces patience."

God Hears Your Prayers

(Psalms 116:1 NIV)

"I love the LORD, for he heard my voice; he heard my cry for mercy."

I was in distress, and fear was growing inside of me. Fear of not being able to ever renounce addiction; fear of not being able to grow and become fruitful; fear of not being able to please God, and voices in my head started to creep in. "You won't make it; it is impossible; God is not listening; you are all alone; no one can't help you; what a weak person you are; you will always be an alcoholic!"

In spite of that, the voices did not stop me from praying and humbling myself before God; instead, I closed my ears to the enemy's lies. When we are getting closer to victory, the enemy creeps in with lies to stop you and distract you. Maybe a friend or a family member is speaking negatively about your struggle. But I, in the name of Jesus, command you to close your ears to enemy lies and negative comments that do not identify you. Open your ears to God's voice and trust in His ways. Though it may seem long and quiet, He is right by your side. The same way He was with me, He will be with you.

One day on a Saturday, there was a lady's service in which there was going to be worship, preaching, and socializing. I was excited, thinking to myself that it was going to be the perfect day for God to finally talk to me. I was enjoying the whole service. I cried and prayed and worship with the hope that God was going to manifest in me. Finally, the lady who was preaching asked all the women to kneel down at the altar and pray for a petition. I said to myself, "Yes, this is the time where God will break silence!" So I went and knelt down on the altar and cried out to God, "Lord, here I am. Please, Father, talk to me. Tell me to stop drinking. Just one word from you, God, is all I need. Please, Lord, do not leave me like this, I am tired of drinking my life away I want to please you." Unfortunately, God did not speak to me, and I left the service disappointed, upset, confused, and sad.

When God doesn't answer you and remains quiet, it doesn't mean that He has forsaken you, that He doesn't love you, or that He is not listening. If you are thinking that God has abandoned you, let's rebuke that thought in Jesus' name because He hasn't! If you meditate on the story of Lazarus who Jesus raised from the dead in John 11:5, you will understand that God comes at the perfect time for His own glory. For us to get to know a different version of Him and for us to see His glory in a time of desperation. The Bible speaks of Lazarus, Martha, and Mary, friends of Jesus who He loved dearly. Jesus was told the news that Lazarus was sick, but yet He remained in the place where He was for two more days. Maybe Martha, the sister of Lazarus, felt like Jesus neglected him. Maybe she thought it was too late for Jesus or did not care about his state, because by the time Jesus got there to Lazarus, he was already dead. But Jesus knows our condition better than ourselves, so He knows the best timing for when to come and save us. In this story Jesus said in John 11:11 (NIV), "Our friend Lazarus has fallen asleep; but I am going there to wake him up." God knows when to come, so we can learn how to believe and have faith even in our darkest time when it seems like His presence is not with us. In John 11:40 (NIV) Jesus said again, "Did I not tell you that if you believe, you will see the glory of God?" So I tell you today, whatever situation you find yourselves in do not be dismayed and have faith because soon you will see the glory of God in your favor.

Resuming my testimony, the next morning of Sunday was the day of my answered prayers. A day I will never forget! I went into church, but this time I was already hopeless and not expecting God to talk to me. While the pastor preached, I felt the sermon in my heart and I cried throughout the sermon. And I remember how he preached stating that some of us want more from God, but we are not willing to go further into the deep and prefer to stay by the seashore. We want to serve God halfway when God wants us to go into a deeper relationship with Him, to delve into the Word of God. Sadly, most of us find ourselves by the seashore afraid to go forward and let God work in us. I felt in my spirit how God prepared the whole sermon for me, so when it was time for the pastor to do the calling for prayers, I suddenly felt afraid to go to the altar. In my heart I felt like it was my time to go forward, but something was stopping me from going. While people started to walk towards the altar for prayers, my heart started to beat fast. I felt like it was going to fall out of my chest. Finally, I decided to go as the last one, after battling if I should go or not. As soon as my pastor placed his hands on me, I started to cry so loud, he started praying for me, telling me how there is an area that I had not yet given up to God, and suddenly, I heard Him say to me, "UNTIL TODAY, GIVE ME THAT TODAY!" I heard a thunderous voice and I knew it was God! Only God knew what I was battling most, only He knew my struggles. God told me to stop today, to give it up! I fell down on my knees with my face on the ground and I cried so loud with such a relief, but also I felt flames of fire running inside me. I felt God's healing, His presence, His hug, His love. He was there right at that moment. He finally answered my prayers and came to save me! That glorious Sunday was the day that I promised God not to touch alcohol again. I knew inside of me that God was there to support me, and it was my time to walk free.

In this process, I learned to be patient, to believe and trust in God, that prayers are answered at the right time. God knows our necessity; He knows our condition more than we do. I had to withdraw from so many things to follow God but let me tell you that what you think is a loss is a gain. Everything that you give up for God is not a loss, it is a gain, and He will return to you more in abundance. Do not be afraid to renounce addictions, habits, or anything for God, because He sees you through the heart, and He will help you, support you, and stand by your side. He will lead you to a better place full of glory ,peace and life.

Are you willing to renounce today? Close your eyes and ask God to help you to renounce those areas, your past, addictions, people, habits, thoughts that do not allow you to deepen your relationship with Him. You no longer want to remain by the seashore but to enter God's divine presence and delve more in the Word and the Gospel. He is willing to help you walk further and guide you as long as you have a willing heart.

Chapter 7

HEALING IN THE DESERT

(Isaiah 43:19 NIV)

"See, I am doing a new thing!

Now it springs up; do you not perceive it? I am making a way in the wilderness and streams in the wasteland."

I love this verse! Such a wonderful, amazing promise from God. When finding yourself spiritually barren, dry and lonely, do not be afraid or dismayed. It is God working His perfect will in you and preparing His way to create a new version of you. See, this is the thing. God works in you by removing all your impurities, healing, restoring, and directing your steps. Once His perfect work reflects on you, His glory will be manifested and everyone shall see it! So behold, because the Lord is an expert at making everything new at a perfect time. Even so, in the middle of God working through us, we all have to go through the seasons of walking through the desert. This is the season that most of us don't like and, sadly, some quit, but I inspire you to continue forward and trust in God because this season of walking in the desert is part of what you are about to become to achieve God's purpose. After I withdrew from fornication, drugs, alcohol, and walked away from my affectionate relationship. God guided me to the desert to form my character, for me to learn how to rely on Him, to bring out that strong warrior that He had deposited in me, to create a new song in my desert, but the best of all was to see His Glory! There is a warrior in you and it will be manifested by overcoming the desert.

What does a desert mean spiritually? For me, it brings thoughts of loneliness, isolation, tears, struggles, discouragement, fear, pain, and battles. But what does the Bible say about the desert? It describes the desert as a solitary place where God reveals Himself to believers. It's a space for intimacy with God, reflection, and drawing closer to Him. It's a time of testing and transformation, where God wants to guide you, teach you, heal you, and lead you to the promised land. Oh, dear one! I have felt that isolation, loneliness, and fear, and I have cried many tears.

When I chose to stop drinking and follow God's will, I didn't realize I would face withdrawal symptoms from alcohol. These symptoms made everything so difficult. I felt tortured daily! My mood swings were intense, I was emotional, and I struggled to work or think clearly. The more I craved alcohol, the weaker I became. I remember calling my mom, crying, saying, "Mom, I can't handle this! I need a margarita; my body is begging for it. I don't know what to do!" In these moments, we must be careful about who we reach out to for help, as not everyone understands our struggles or what God is doing in our lives. Be cautious! God wants you to seek Him, especially in your darkest times. He will listen and give you strength!

While I experienced the withdrawal symptoms, my body hurt, my hands trembled, and I felt chills. I was overwhelmed with loneliness and desperation. Everything around me felt dark, and I was confused. I asked God, "If you want me to stop drinking, why am I feeling this way?" It felt like I was suffering alone without His help. Every day was filled with discouragement. Withdrawal is tough. Honestly, it weakens your body, but now I see it was worth it. God helped me through this. He never puts you in a situation you can't handle. Whatever you're facing today, God knows you can overcome it. When things get tough, He gives you strength so you can see His glory. I didn't understand this back then, so I struggled with withdrawal and the urge to drink again. At family gatherings, I would leave because I couldn't be around alcohol. This made it harder, as I distanced myself from my family to avoid temptation. Avoiding them made me feel even lonelier. Choosing to follow Jesus in a place where no one else does can be frustrating and isolating. But I learned that loneliness can be necessary! It's not a bad thing; it's a blessing because it allows you to connect with God and understand yourself better. So in the season of being in the wilderness, it was just me! No one knew what I was battling at home, no one saw my tears, no one saw me sick, no one saw my desperation, but God! One day, when I was working from home, I sat down on my computer and I bust out crying. I started to yell so loudly and said, "God I quit, I can't do this! It is too painful. I did not sign in for this. I prefer to go back where I came from where I can just drink and numb myself." And that is when thoughts of quitting filled my mind. Minutes later, I picked up my phone to call my pastor's wife and tell her that I wouldn't be returning to church. Okay, I know it sounds crazy that after everything I went through I wanted to surrender and go back! But this is a process that a lot of us go through in the walk of faith. When God frees us and guides us to the desert to mold us, it hurts so much that we just want to give up because we just want the easy way out. When we face something new, we feel afraid, and we start to look back.

In the story of how God used Moses to free the Israelites from Egypt, they found themselves in the desert facing a big change in their lives. As they walked for days, feeling scared, confused, and tired, they complained to Moses, wishing they had died in Egypt instead. Despite their complaints, God showed great mercy by sending down bread from heaven to feed them.

Why share this? Just as God was with the Israelites in the desert, hearing their cries and meeting their needs, He is with you too! This shows the true nature of God: He is good, merciful, loving, and caring. As long as you are following His purpose, He will not abandon you. Do not give up! In your desert, do not throw in the towel! The desert is not meant to harm you or make you go back; it is a time to keep your eyes on the cross and allow God to fulfill His perfect plan for you. I promise you; everything will be alright! God is with you, He hasn't left you, and He never will. Take a moment to reflect on Romans 8:18 (NIV), which says, "I consider that our present sufferings are not worth comparing with the glory that will be revealed in us." Your current struggles are part of a journey leading to joy and glory, so keep smiling and stay hopeful!

In the process of picking up my phone to call my pastor's wife I heard a voice inside of me demanding me to go to my room to cry out to the Lord. So I obediently left the phone on my desk and walked to my room, closed the doors, fell on my knees, lifted up my eyes, and cried out, "Lord I can't anymore, this walk has been so tiring, I feel weak, drained, alone, confused. I am in despair, I just can't handle this anymore, I am being tempted. I am sick. If you don't come to save me I will perish today! If you don't do something, I give up today!" And so I cried, and cried, and cried until I felt a resting, peaceful spirit. My tears felt as if they were being wiped out, and my weakness turned into a new strength. And this is how I realized that God was teaching me how to lean on Him, that there is time when He just wants us to cry out to Him for help and He will respond.

When feeling tired, like giving up, instead of thinking your way out, prepare the way for the Lord! He will give you rivers of living water in your season of drought. God's living water is a nourishment and a healing to our soul, is a water that we all need in order not to thirst again. Jesus once told a Samaritan woman in John 4:13-14 (NIV), "Everyone who drinks this water will be thirsty again, but whoever drinks the water I give them will never thirst. Indeed, the water I give them will become in them a spring of water welling up to eternal life."

That same day, it was time to go to church, and I decided to walk forward for prayer, looking for God's instructions in this hard time. Through the pastor, God asked me to fast for three days. I remember walking out of church saying to myself, "Is God serious? He wants me to fast for three days, how am I supposed to do that?" I will be honest, I did believe in the power of fasting, but I never made it part of my spiritual life because I thought fasting was hard, and I just love to eat! But it was time for me to change my way of thinking and allow God to guide me. If I wanted changes in my life, I needed to be obedient and have a change of mentality! Obedience is the key to God's purpose! Even if we don't understand why God is asking us to do something, we need to have confidence in Him because only God knows us more than we do. Obedience to God opens door's that you could have thought were impossible!

So I fasted. I separated three days for God, and I presented to Him my temptations, my worries, my burdens. Fasting is such a powerful resource that God has empowered us with. I realize after the three days of fasting I was no longer tempted, I was cured of alcohol withdrawal, my body was not craving it anymore, and I was happier and joyful. My body regained the strength that I needed to keep moving forward. There are a lot of reason you can fast, but in this case, I fasted for internal healing and freedom. After those three days of fasting, I got back up. I was able to focus more on my life, on myself, and on my relationship with God. But it doesn't end here! Serving God is a journey. A journey of discovering who God really is, a journey of internal healing, a journey of removing, of cleansing, and of discovering your purpose (which we will be discussing in the next chapter) but overall, it is a path of allowing God's perfect work to be done in you. Have you felt since you started this journey that maybe friends or family are not supporting you? Maybe you don't get calls from them like before? Or not getting invited to go out as usual? Well, as hard as it seems, it is good news! That means they are seeing a change in you! God is removing people that can't be part of where He is taking you. This is something I have learned in my process; when those family or friends closer to you see your testimony God starts working through them too! But first we need to let go and let God!

HEALING

(Psalm 147:3 NIV)

"He heals the brokenhearted and binds up their wounds."

I have to say that in this chapter I had to pause from writing. I all of a sudden felt stuck and had no words. I couldn't understand what was wrong with me, so I paused preparing this book and searched for God's answers. I prayed and told God, "If this book is your will, if my testimony should be heard, why am I stuck now in this chapter? Why suddenly do I feel sad, and my spirit feels broken and contrite?" I will be honest with you, I couldn't understand what was going on inside of me, so I gave myself a break from writing.

I started to wake up feeling sorrowful and with my heart broken, but I couldn't understand why. Then the past of my relationship with the father of my daughter started to haunt me at night, and insomnia started to knock at my door. On Christmas day, I told my aunt Kevelyn, "I'm feeling sad, but I don't understand why."

A day didn't go by without asking God to lead me to an understanding of what was wrong with my heart. I felt such a huge burden and sadness which stopped me from writing. But then I understood that God wanted me to pause because He needed to remove impurities that I still had left in my heart. And this is what happens to most of us. This is part of the healing journey when God has to confront us with an internal pain that we are holding on to without realizing it. This is the process of internal healing and removing impurities. I couldn't start writing about healing without being fully healed. You can't move on to your purpose without being fully healed! There are deep wounds inside our hearts that we try to cover and hide, but God has to confront us and start the process of refinement. In case if you don't know the meaning of refinement, it is the process of removing impurities. The Bible says in Zechariah 13:9, "This third I will put into the fire; I will refine them like silver and test them like gold. They will call on my name and I will answer them."

Are you struggling right now with a feeling of deep sadness? Does your spirit feel contrite? Have you lost the desire to keep going? Does every day feel senseless with no purpose? If you have been feeling discouraged, lost, empty, sorrowful, and not understanding why, then I will answer that for you. God is trying to confront an area in your heart that you have been holding on to. A painful past, grief from a miscarriage, grief from an abortion, a grudge, the feeling of losing someone, wounds, bitterness, lack of forgiveness, or disappointment. Whatever it is, God wants to refine you like silver!

In the book of Malachi 3:3 (NIV), it says, "He will sit as a refiner and purifier of silver." When refining, the silver has to be placed in the hottest flames of fire to burn out impurities (a process in which God removes impurities and contamination out of our hearts), but while this is happening, the refiner sits in front of the fire the whole entire time while the silver is being refined, making sure the flames don't destroy it. While God is refining you, the process will surely hurt, but He is right beside you throughout the steps of refinement. He won't allow the fire to burn you but to turn you into a refined silver that reflects Him in it. God is holy with a clean, loving heart. For us to move forward, our hearts must be transformed and purified. Remember, that God is sitting right next to you to prepare you for a bigger season of your life!

On a Tuesday night of Bible class, the pastor's wife spoke of how it is important for us to remain in the vine as the branches. Jesus is the Vine and we are the branches, the Bible says apart from Him we can do nothing, we can't produce fruits. However, we need to reflect on the areas that don't allow us to remain in the vine and prevent us from producing fruits. I reflected that night, and I left the Bible class crying on my way home because I felt God touching my heart and confronting me that it was time to let go of the hidden pain I was holding on to. That pain was surfacing and causing me to feel a burden, emptiness, and sadness in my heart. I realized that it was surfacing because

God wanted me to LET GO and LET HIM work on it. I got home, I wept and admitted to God that though I let go of my relationship with my EX-boyfriend physically and verbally, I did not let him go from my heart. I was still in resentment, not understanding why he chose the world instead of fighting to save our family. I was suffering a loss of an unwanted goodbye. I was in grief but tried to cover it and by trying to cover it led to sadness and a burden that I no longer wanted to carry. I wept the whole night and asked God to remove this from my heart and to help me forgive him. I told God that the pain was unbearable, I alone couldn't heal myself. Let me pause right here and ask you a question: "What have you lost in life and what caused it?" In this life we can suffer losses and unwanted goodbyes, such as the death of a loved one, a break up, the loss of a job, loss of a house, infirmities, or childhood traumas that cause us to lose part of our lives. All this can cause a root of grief in our hearts.

(James 5:15 NIV)

"And the prayer offered in faith will make the sick person well; the Lord will raise them up."

That same night of weeping and confessing to God my deepest hidden emotions that were buried in my heart for two years, I fell asleep. While I slept with my face down on my pillow, I felt a presence that lay on my back and hugged me. But what intrigued me the most was the feeling of a hand that passed through my heart. I felt a hand grabbing my heart and repositioning it while I slept. I suddenly woke up with the sensation of a hand grabbing my heart and I looked at the time, and it was 4:00 am. I felt such a calm, peaceful, and glorious atmosphere in my room. I heard a voice telling me, "Rest in peace, I am right here with you is going to be okay," but I was so astonished to realize that the burden I was carrying in my heart was totally gone and was replaced with joy. I woke up hours later with such happiness and joy. Right at that moment, I understood that God was waiting for me to confess, to open up to Him to what was really bothering me for so long for Him to heal me.

I had to share this great part of the testimony that happened to me while working on this chapter, because I believe that God wants to heal you in your season of walking through the wilderness. Your most inner emotions and pain will start to surface because that is where God wants to enter to restore you and make you new. God wants to hug you and fill you up with joy and take away that burden that has been in your heart for so long that won't let you remain in the vine. When we remain in God, He remains in us, and He can heal and restore us so we can produce fruits. The fruits that will help us cross to the next level, fruits that will make us multiply and spread the love and joy of God. Jesus want to comfort you today! He is sitting right next to you, open up your heart to Him right now and confess to Him your deep emotions that have been buried for a long time.

The Desert Is Necessary

When being guided to the desert by God, it is not for us to suffer, to be dismayed, feel abandoned, or lose hope and faith, but is to transform our character, to renew our minds, to prepare us for His purpose and to get to know Him more. The desert is like a training camp, where we learn how to trust, believe, and depend on God and train with the resources He has equipped us with. The same way soldiers train to fight their opponents, just like that God trains us to overcome and resist our adversaries. When we enter the desert, we don't enter empty-handed. God has given us powerful tools, such as the Word, worship, praise, prayers, and fasting. Without God's words, nothing can be accomplished: we need the word of God for guidance, to be filled; we need prayers to communicate; we need praise to express our gratitude and rejoice in Him. As long as His presence goes with us, we are more than equipped. In Exodus 33 (NIV) Moses said, "If you don't personally go with us, don't make us leave this place." Now tell God today, "if your presence is with me, that is all I need! If you don't go with me, do not move me from here! Hallelujah! Because if, with you, I go through the rivers, it will not sweep me over and, if I walk through the fire, I won't be burned because you, God, you are my helper, my protector, my rock and my fortress."

In our time of experiencing our spiritual desert, we can run towards confusion, mixed emotions, doubts, loneliness, depression, desperation, losses, sorrow, criticism, offenses, grief, and strong decisions. Are you facing one of these today?

At the beginning of this chapter, I mentioned that the desert to me meant LONELINESS. God wants to embrace you with His presence. I also mentioned TEARS. God wants to collect your tears today! Oh, but I also stated BATTLES. God wants to make you a warrior! I mentioned TRIALS. God wants to test your heart and refine it. I also stated FEARS. God wants you to trust in Him. I said DISCOURAGEMENT and TIREDNESS. God wants to strengthen your faith. PAIN. God wants to heal you! It doesn't matter what you are facing today because in every storm the sun will rise! light will shine soon in your storm! Jesus is your light! God will never leave you, the same way He was with Moses, the same way He will be with you. Moses told the people "Don't be afraid. Just stand still and watch the LORD rescue you today. The Egyptians you see today will never be seen again." Let me preach it to you in rice and beans, whatever circumstances your facing today, DO NOT FEAR, and remain still trusting that God is working everything out in your life to rescue you and lead you to the promise land (to your purpose), and those difficult moments of your life, situation, enemies, financial stability, diseases, addiction, rejections, wounds, brokenness, depression, anxiety, and loneliness that you have been struggling with, YOU WILL NOT AGAIN SEE IT! Because the Lord is writing a new chapter, doing something new in your life, filling dry empty areas of your heart and opening a path in the impossible.

From this chapter I want you to focus on these areas:

1. Don't look back.

2. There is nothing waiting for you in Egypt.

3. Do not quit.

4. Stop complaining and trust God.

5. Let go and let God.

6. Confess to God your innermost pain.

7. God is your refiner.

8. The desert is necessary to develop the character of God, to prepare for the next level, to experience God like never before, and to develop a relationship of trust and hope.

9. What had you enslaved, you will never see again.

10. God is writing a new chapter of your life.

Chapter 8

Your Identity

(1 Peter 2:9 NIV)

"But you are a chosen people, a royal priesthood, a holy nation, God's special possession, that you may declare the praises of him who called you out of darkness into his wonderful light."

Wow! What an intense chapter we just came from! I don't know what your wilderness is looking like to you, but I am certain that finding your true identity in Christ helps you overcome any obstacle in this world and any attack of the enemy. This is one of the biggest concerns and dilemmas we are dealing with today: knowing who we are in Christ. So many people are wandering around without purpose, without direction and without an idea of who they are! This is one of the biggest areas where Satan attacks God's people, leading to identity crisis. But YOU! Yes YOU! It is time to look at yourself how God look's at you! You are His special possession. Do you know what that means? Have you ever held on to something that is so special to you? You try to keep it safe and protect it so that no one else can touch it or damage it, because you own it, it belongs to you, and you have feelings for it. That is exactly how God see us; we are His property, His creation, we are His image, in His eyes we are precious and honored, we are His heir, He see us with good purpose, but the best of all, He sees us cleansed, pure, and holy through the blood of His Son that was shed on the cross. That blood that runs through us has cleansed us and made us new, a new creature in Christ. We are no longer of this world but from the kingdom of God. We are no longer wanderers, lost, or a puppet of the enemy because now we are ambassadors (representatives, messengers) of Christ. We live for Christ because He lives in us! We are His temple! So position yourself as a child of God, your posture is not to remain stuck living in the dark but to walk out and be the LIGHT that God is calling you to be because now you don't walk alone, now the Holy Spirit is by your side guiding you to SHINE! Just like God created nature (flowers, trees, plants) to blossom, to sprout, and to produce fruits, YOU were also called to blossom, to sprout, and to be fruitful for His Glory.

Life was not meant to be easy, but I learned during the hard challenging times I must remain standing and productive, but what keeps me standing and productive is knowing my identity in Christ! Identity crisis happens to almost all of us, and for so long I struggled with it because of my past experiences, traumas, childhood, and hardships. I used to feel inferior, insignificant, defective, and purposeless. Except that I only felt that way because I did not have knowledge of the plans that God already had planned for me in eternity. Let's read Psalm 139:16 (NIV), which says the following, "Your eyes saw my unformed body; all the days ordained for me were written in your book before one of them came to be." In other words, in eternity a word was already spoken about you, there is a plan (agenda) that has been prepared for you in eternity! However, I allowed God to renew my mind, and my heart with His words, His love and grace. The same way He worked with me I believe that He will work with you too, because you too are His CHOSEN BELOVED!

(Ephesians 2:10 NIV)

"For we are God's handiwork, created in Christ Jesus to do good works, which God prepared in advance for us to do."

You are a unique creation of God! Don't let your past, mistakes, struggles, pain, culture, traumas, or weaknesses define you! The labels that others or society may have given you (like crazy, orphan, useless, drunkard, sinner, barren, addict, etc.) do not define your true self! You are wonderfully made by a skilled Creator. You are beautiful because you were made for good purposes. Recognizing who you are and how Christ views you gives you strength. Your identity comes from understanding and believing that the powerful, eternal God lives within you and allowing Him to change and renew your mind. The mind is incredibly powerful; what we think shapes our actions, how we present ourselves, how we speak, and how we behave. If you think negatively about everything, about yourself and others, that is what your eyes will see. What you believe about yourself, whatever thought you allow to control your mind, will control your life and future because you are allowing it to influence you. What is in your mind leads your heart and the heart reflects your life.

A Little of My History

For so long I had struggled with my identity. I always felt like an outcast, a loser, like the ugly sheep of the family, unfit for this world. When I was young, I had a rough childhood just like most of us. I know what it is to grow up in an environment of violence, seeing your mom being mistreated and not being able to do anything, and going to sleep feeling afraid. An environment with bottles of alcohol surrounding you, nights with parties and people all the time in the house and not being able to sleep to go to school because the music in the living room was so loud that even the walls trembled. I experience growing up with only my mom and little brother, struggling to pay rent, having a beach cooler instead of a fridge, sometimes days without light in the house. I remember walking in cold snowy days to school not wanting to go because I was tired of being bullied. In the school bathroom girls would yelled at me, at recess I would be told how ugly I dressed, and on the way to school being followed and smacked on the head. I always had in mind one question, "Why do I even exist?" But locking myself in my room and writing was my way out from the physical world. Writing was my passion; it relieved my heart when feeling alone and scared. There was a time in my life in which my mom was in such a depression and struggling economically, she had no choice but to send me and my brother to Puerto Rico to live with my grandmother. Those months in Puerto Rico, I became rebellious and hot tempered because I missed my mom and dad so much. I had so much anger in me.

I started drinking when I was thirteen years old. I would take my mom's small can of beers and hide them under the pillow and drink it at night, staring outside my window searching for hope. In my teenage years I started to experience real depression. I once went into the bathroom, took a bottle of pills, and swallowed it with the intention to die. Luckily, my mom's friend was able to rush me to the hospital where they had to place an ECG on my chest. I remember my mom's friend on the phone with my mom telling her, "You need to come, your daughter is not well," and once my mom got there, seeing her tears made me regret what I had done. When I started high school, I became more depressed and rebellious but I was suffering alone in silence. I started to hurt myself on my arms because I realized that cutting myself felt like a relief to the pain I was already experiencing inside of me. Moving to Florida I thought it was going to be better from what I was already going through in New Jersey but actually that is where I really lost myself. Moving to Florida my mother still struggled economically so she had to work both day and night. I already did not have my dad physically because he was living in New Jersey, and my brother was no longer with me because he decided to stay with my dad. So not having my dad or my brother around, and my mom having to work all the time, I felt alone and free to do whatever I wanted. I refuged myself in the streets with friends, drinking every day, smoking, doing drugs, and partying, I was coming home late and skipping school. I really thought this was life. I thought what I was doing was fun, but in reality I was just hiding my pain. People called me names: the troublemaker, the drunkard, crazy, and much worse. My friends' mothers didn't want them with me because of how I used to conduct myself, always with a bottle of alcohol in my hands, and the way I used to dress provocatively. My mom was always busy, from her day job to then go to work at nighttime at the bar. So when I turned eighteen I also started working at a bar. There I was able to experience the drug environment, consumed it mixing it with alcohol and passing out on tables. I even participated in helping to sell it for extra money. And it was there that I totally didn't know who I was anymore. The easy money blinded my eyes, the drugs cured my pain temporarily. I started to believe what everyone said about me, "YOU will never make it out, who works in a bar stays in the bar, who enters the world of drugs never gets out." I believed the voices in my head that I was a nobody, no one loved me or cared for me.

I am not telling this story of myself for you to pity me, but to see that in my darkest moments God already had a plan. Maybe you can relate to some of this, but I tell you this: you are NOT your past. You are NOT what people say you are, you are what GOD says you are. Every story has a purpose, and your life is not meaningless or a waste, your life is a PURPOSE planned by God.

(Jeremiah 1:5 NIV)

"Before I formed you in the womb I knew you, before you were born I set you apart; I appointed you as a prophet to the nations."

Today, at this very moment, the Lord wants you to understand that He knew you even before you were created. You were already in His thoughts, and you were loved by Him first. To discover your identity, it's important to realize that God loved you, thought of you, set you apart, and had a wonderful purpose for you. You are not here by mistake; you are part of God's perfect plan. I later realized that my past shaped who I am today. My experiences made me stronger and even when I felt alone I now see that God was always by my side, guiding me to Him. One part of this message that stands out to me is when it says, "I set you apart." Have you ever wondered why loneliness visits you? Why do some nights feel so empty? Why do friends and family sometimes leave when you need them most? It's because God has set you apart. When something is set apart, it is seen as valuable and unique, with special qualities that should be protected. Finding your identity in Christ often means spending time alone, as you can't always be around people who don't share the same vision. There are those who may want you to follow their path, but as Christians, we are meant to be different. We should reflect God's character, love, peace, joy, and patience, as we are called to serve. It's easy to let others lead us down a harmful path if we aren't strong in our faith. While we are set apart, God is helping us grow in His character and spirit. In times of loneliness, there is also silence where God is at work, transforming you and preparing something new within you. These moments allow you to focus on God, who has called you to reveal your identity in Him. There may be people or things in your life that hold you back from discovering who you really are.

In Exodus chapter 3, Moses was part of the Egyptian royal family before he realized he was a Hebrew and understood his true calling. He would not have discovered his identity if he hadn't fled Egypt. He escaped after killing an Egyptian who was mistreating a Hebrew slave, which led the Pharaoh to seek his life. This speaks to me because we all face challenges and pain that can help us understand our identity in Christ. After fleeing, Moses spent years feeling lost until he encountered God in a burning bush. In that moment, he was alone, and God revealed his purpose to free the Hebrews from their suffering. During your quiet time with God, He wants to show Himself to you and guide you toward His will. He desires a closer relationship with you and wants to transform you into a new version of yourself. In Exodus 3:5 (NIV), God told Moses. "Take off your sandals, for the place where you are standing is holy ground." This represents the necessity of letting go of your former self to embrace the new identity that He has designed for you. Prior to Moses joining the royal family, his mother protected him by placing him in a basket, aware that he was destined for a significant purpose. Similarly, God has a distinct plan for your life. To discover it, you must surrender your life to Jesus, refresh your mind each day with His teachings, worship Him, and dedicate time to be in His presence.

When I found myself in defeat, dragged into the pit of depression where all I saw was darkness with no way out. I wept and wept and drank until feeling hopeless and dead within myself. One sunny day I sat in my back yard, opened the Bible, and started to talk to God, just me and Him. While I read the Word of God, I started to see the word "Identity" in my mind. There I understood God was telling me that my posture was not the posture of defeat but the posture of being in His presence, where I can recover what I had lost, my identity, and after that I started to tell myself everyday looking in the mirror, "I am a child of God and I belong to God. I am a somebody. I am His beloved daughter, I have identity in Christ!" Having one on one time with God, reading His Word, and declaring His words and promises upon myself helped me recover what Satan had snatched away from me: my life, my peace, and my joy! Declaring, believing, and putting to practice the Word of God helped me conquer the depression and the anxiety who had been my companions for so long. Recovering my identity in Christ also helped me to be free from drugs and alcohol because I knew that God was calling me and it was time to leave everything behind and follow Him. God is calling you, my friend! Only in Christ you can find your identity and purpose. There is no other way, nothing in this world that can reveal to you your real purpose and true self, only the God that created you, formed you, and set you apart! Being alone with God is the key to your true self, to the new you! You cannot be your purpose without identity! The enemy will rise against you, he will use others against you, your family might be against you, the whole world might rise against you but remain still. God told Moses in Exodus 3:12 (NIV), "I will be with you." This promise is also for you, receive it in your heart: "I will be with you!" Declare it, believe it, and walk in your purpose!

I want to inspire you today to not let your weaknesses, past mistakes, or former identity hinder you from pursuing the path that God has laid out for you. Perfection is unattainable for anyone in this world! Life can be challenging, but it is through these trials and tribulations that we grow stronger and more mature. One of the aspects I admire most about Jesus is that He selected twelve disciples, each of whom had their own flaws. Peter, for instance, was quick-tempered and denied Jesus three times, yet this did not prevent Jesus from realizing His purpose through Peter. Judas betrayed Him, but even then, Jesus offered him bread and a cup during the Last Supper. The Apostle Paul, originally known as Saul, was a persecutor of the church, yet he was chosen to spread the Gospel to the Gentiles, kings, and the children of Israel. Moses, who struggled with a speech impediment and had committed murder, was still chosen to lead the Israelites to freedom. Rahab, a woman with a troubled past, played a crucial role in protecting Joshua's spies, demonstrating her faith and courage, which ultimately saved her and her family. Queen Esther, an orphan, was elevated to royalty and used her position to save her people. Jonah initially fled from God's calling and even wished for death in his anger, but that did not stop God from transforming his heart and using him for His purpose. The Bible is filled with stories that resonate with our imperfect humanity, highlighting the necessity of Jesus in our lives to accomplish His perfect work within us. God delights in showcasing His power and glory through those who have faced rejection, ridicule, and hardship, crafting them into masterpieces for His purpose. Through you, God seeks to save lives, heal, restore, and communicate His message. He desires to demonstrate that He is the one true God, and that the only way to Him is through Jesus. You have been CHOSEN by God! Do not view yourself as unworthy or lacking purpose. Instead of allowing the opinions of others to define you, choose to place your hope and faith in God, who takes joy in you. "God takes pleasure in those who honor Him, trust Him, and place their hope in His unwavering love." Additionally, I want to remind you that by accepting Jesus as your Savior, you have been redeemed. You have regained life, purpose, and identity at a cost that no one else could have paid for you.

(Ephesians 1:7 NIV)

"In him we have redemption through his blood, the forgiveness of sins, in accordance with the riches of God's grace."

Here she stands, the young woman who once wept herself to sleep, feeling utterly hopeless and adrift. She was engulfed in darkness, bound by invisible chains, seeking solace in men, alcohol, and drugs. She fought against depression and struggled with feelings of abandonment, often feeling unloved, rejected, and unappreciated. Those she cherished criticized and betrayed her. Yet, it is this very woman who is now penning this book, guided by the Holy Spirit that dwells within her, providing her with companionship and direction. Through grace and the mercy of God, she has emerged victorious, discovering her identity. Now is the moment for you to rise, lift your head, and walk in alignment with God's purpose!

Summarizing this chapter:

1. When you understand your identity in Christ, no one and nothing can take away what God has already declared over you.

2. God set you apart and chose you for a unique purpose even before your creation.

3. You were cherished by God long before you were conceived.

4. Your thoughts shape your actions, so avoid allowing negative thinking to dominate your mind.

5. Experiencing loneliness is essential for personal growth, preparation, and developing a relationship with God.

6. Perfection is unattainable; however, God uses our imperfections to fulfill His purpose.

7. Your history does not define you; rather, it serves to strengthen you.

8. To walk in your purpose, you must first understand your identity.

9. Declare, believe, and actively practice the teachings of God.

10. Pursue God and cultivate a deeper connection with Him.

11. Acknowledge your worth and uniqueness in the eyes of God.

12. By placing your trust and hope in Him, you will fulfill the purpose and assignments He has for you.

13. With God's power, strength, and love, you will rise above criticism and opposition.

14. Recognizing your identity makes you a formidable adversary to the enemy.

Remain vigilant, for the adversary's conflict with you stems from his awareness of your distinct, inherent design: one that he once possessed but subsequently corrupted. His aim is to sow confusion and doubt regarding your identity in God, knowing that he cannot take away your unique design; only you have the power to do so. The enemy has already been vanquished, yet you still have the chance to embrace your divine calling and walk with intention.

I pray that this chapter and the Word of God guide you toward your true identity in Christ and unlock the doors to your purpose in this life. May the Scriptures fortify you, providing peace, direction, joy, and assurance on your journey. I hope that your exceptional design remains untainted by the enemy's schemes, serving as a testament to the Living God. From the depths of my heart, I pray that you no longer permit the past to interfere with your purpose, that the hurtful words and moments of sorrow cease to define you. I pray that you, holding this book, recognize yourself as a child of God, destined for a significant mission on this earth. You are beautiful, valuable, and a warrior in Christ. In Jesus' name, I declare that today marks the beginning of your purpose, that you will grow in prayer and deepen your relationship with the Holy Spirit like never before. A new version of you will emerge today in Jesus' name, complete with a new identity and purpose, and no one will be able to take it away from you. I declare it accomplished by the power of Jesus' name.

A new identity and purpose emerge today! Embrace it, have faith in it, and put it into action!

Chapter 9

DO NOT FEAR THE UNKNOWN

(Romans 8:15 NIV)

"For you did not receive a spirit that makes you a slave again to fear, but you received the Spirit of sonship. And by Him we cry, 'Abba, Father.'"

Fear is an emotion that everyone experiences, and it is not a sin to feel afraid. However, as children of God, we must not permit fear to dominate our daily lives and emotions. I chose to address the topic of fear because it is one of the most significant tools that Satan employs against God's children, aiming to render us paralyzed, doubtful, unproductive, and confined to our comfort zones. I understand that confronting new challenges and placing our trust in the unseen can be daunting. This is where faith becomes essential, as it allows us to believe in our hearts what we cannot perceive. The beauty of this journey is that through our relationship with God, we can find peace and not fear what tomorrow may bring. We can rest peacefully at night, entrusting all our concerns to Him. Regardless of our actions or destinations, God has promised to accompany us as we walk in

His purpose, as stated in Matthew 28:20 (NIV), "And surely I am with you always, to the very end of the age."

Serving God can often feel enigmatic and, at times, intimidating, as we may be uncertain about the direction in which we are being led. The surprises that await us can be unpredictable, as God's intentions and plans surpass our own understanding. While we may envision a particular path, God may redirect us, saying, "Not this way, try another route!"

Many individuals hesitate to serve God, often burdened by negative self-perceptions such as "I am not worthy" or "I can't overcome my habits like smoking or drinking." They may think, "It seems difficult; I will likely fail Him again." If these thoughts resonate with you, remember that God is already aware of the intentions of our hearts. Despite knowing our struggles and shortcomings, He chose to sacrifice Himself on the cross for us because He has a purpose for each of us. You should never feel that you must be fully prepared to serve God, as that state may never be achieved. Serving Him is a journey of faith, where you trust in the Father, grow each day, and even when you stumble, He will be there to lift you up once more. The book of Proverbs 24:16 (NIV) says, "For though the righteous fall seven times, they rise again." What really matters is that you DO NOT stay in that condition, you GET UP again and keep going forward. Hard times create strong people, because it is how we mature in character and learn to trust in God no matter how hard or bad the trial is. In my five years of serving Christ I have failed, felt discouraged and afraid, I have been hurt, felt alone, and almost felt close to giving up. But thanks to that hard season, I was able to experience the mercy and the strength of God. From every hurtful and scary experience I grew in faith, in the Word, and in my relationship with the Holy Spirit. That is what God wants for you too! This path of faith, of being a follower of Christ and leaving everything behind, it's not easy. You will experience all types of emotions (sadness, happiness, fear, everything from joy to mourning, discouragement, tiredness, excitement, weakness) but what's most important is to go through it with the Holy Spirit by your side and not allow the emotions to control you. When we learn to master our emotions we become mature and there we gain the victory! Because the enemy can no longer use fear or discouragement against you! Overcome fear with hope! With hope placed on the promises of God upon your life, hold on to God in any hardships, in the midst of not understanding Gods plan or even when you feel like you are swimming against the current of a river. seek God as your anchor. The Bible says in Hebrew 6:10 (NIV), "We have this hope as an anchor for the soul, firm and secure." Do not be afraid to follow God without direction, because God's ways and paths are trustworthy and better than ours, they are for our good. One of my favorite books, Proverbs 23:26 (NIV), says the following, "My son, give me your heart and let your eyes delight in my ways."

When we dig into the story of Abraham in Genesis 12, known then as Abram, we can understand in verse 4 that Abraham lived in Haran with his family. In Genesis 12:1 (NIV) God called Abram: "The Lord had said to Abram, 'Go from your country, your people and your father's household to the land I will show you.'" And Abram followed the voice of God. God is seeking people who will follow His voice, who can walk forward and leave their old lives behind, a person who is decisive without thinking twice. Abram did not stand there to think about it, he just grabbed his belonging and his family and walked to the unknown. Here I asked myself, "What does the voice of God have that made him so obedient and decisive?" Are you asking yourself that as well? Well that voice was the Holy spirit of God, the same spirit that is within you, the same spirit that guides you to all truth, the same spirit in Genesis 1 who was hovering over the waters creating the heavens and earth with God. I do believe that the spirit of God guided Abram to do the will of the Father. Now let me ask you: Are you willing to follow the voice of God? There is a voice inside of you telling you, "Follow me to where I am taking you." Now are you going to be decisive? Do you know what decisive means? The definition of decisive is "making decisions quickly based on the perfect will of God." There are decisions that we have to make urgently, because our family and generations depend on that decision. In Genesis 12:3-7 God promised Abram that He will bless him with a great nation, that He will bless people through him, and that his land will belong to his offspring. This promise is also yours if you decide to follow God's will. There are people waiting for you to bless them with what God has deposited in you! There is a nation waiting to hear you, waiting for you to lead them to the truth! And your generation to come depends on what you decide to do today! What you sow today, what you decide to do today for God, that inheritance can be passed on to your future generations, for example opening the doors of salvation for generations to come. How beautiful is that? You marking the difference in your family, breaking generational curses, bringing life because you decided to follow the voice of God. I will give you the key that has made me successful when feeling afraid and discouraged, and that key is reminding God in my prayers of His promise to me, reminding myself constantly of the Word that God has placed upon me. If I decide to quit and leave it all, my family and generations will be in danger. Again what you decide to do today, your family and generations depends on! If this story was not enough let me give you another biblical story.

Genesis 24 recounts the story of a woman named Rebekah, who is the daughter-in-law of Abraham. As Abraham aged, he instructed his servant to find a suitable wife for his son Isaac. Upon reaching Nahor, the servant sought divine guidance and prayed that the woman who offered both him and his camels water would be the one chosen for Isaac. Remarkably, this is exactly what transpired; the servant, demonstrating obedience and faith, successfully fulfilled his mission. When Rebekah learned of this, she immediately accepted and hurried to her family home, where they welcomed Abraham's servant. Imagine yourself in Rebekah's position: a young girl living with her family, engaged in daily household tasks, perhaps routinely drawing water, and cherishing moments spent with her family and brother. In Genesis 24:55 (NIV), her mother and brother expressed their desire for her to stay a little longer, saying, "But her brother and her mother replied, 'Let the young woman remain with us ten days or so; then you may go.'" This woman's life transformed dramatically from one day to the next. Once dedicated to her family, she now faced the prospect of traveling great distances to an unfamiliar land to meet her future husband, whom she had never encountered before. This is what I call a journey to the unknown. Perhaps you find yourself in a similar situation, going about your daily routine and concentrating on various aspects of your life, yet now you feel a divine call to venture into the unknown. I am inspired by Rebekah's response in Genesis 24:58 (NIV), where she simply stated, "I will go." This reflects her decisiveness and trust in God. As a woman, I can imagine she may have experienced sadness at leaving her family and apprehension about traveling with a stranger to marry someone she had never met. However, her courage is commendable; she surrendered herself to God and allowed Him to guide her journey. Are you prepared to confront your fears and respond to the Lord with "I will go"? Avoid fixating on the uncertainties or the obstacles in your path. The journey of faith is not meant to be navigated by sight but by hope and trust. It is natural to fear the unknown and to step into uncharted territory, yet God is the one who directs our steps. As stated in Proverbs 20:24 (NIV), "A person's steps are directed by the LORD. How then can anyone understand their own way?" Remember, God orchestrates everything in His way for His glory.

If Abraham and Rebekah had let fear and doubt take over their minds and hearts, they would have missed out on what God had in store for them. Abraham had a land and a nation waiting for him, while Rebekah had a husband ready to welcome her. The enemy doesn't want you to succeed; he wants to keep your family and future generations from being saved. He doesn't want YOU to make an impact in this world, so he'll use fear and doubt as his biggest weapons to weaken you and make you want to give up. I've been there too, facing my own giants of fear and doubt. The toughest giant you'll ever face is actually yourself! I've struggled with insecurities, being in the spotlight, public speaking, worrying about what others think, and questioning my purpose and abilities. But look at me now! I'm still here, trusting in God's plan for my life. I still get a bit nervous when I'm in the spotlight, but there's something my pastor, Christian, said that really stuck with me and helped me push through my fears. He told me, "When you're scared to do what God has called you to do, remind yourself that you were born for this!" So today, let's tackle that fear that tries to hold us back and declare, "I was born for this!" Sometimes, we can be our own worst enemies, dwelling on past failures and thinking we can't become who God wants us to be. Maybe God is calling you to be a pastor, an evangelist, a singer, a writer, a teacher, a healer, or even a prophet for this nation—the possibilities are endless because God doesn't put limits on us. You might feel like you lack the skills or strength to pursue these callings, but if you choose to stand up against your fears and let God's word transform your mindset, you can become whatever He has planned for you! I remember chatting with my pastor's wife, Nora, just before a service, telling her how nervous I was about speaking. She looked at me with both kindness and seriousness and said, "Maybe you're feeling insecure, and that's something you need to work on." Those words hit me hard, but in a good way—it was like a light bulb went off. I started to think, "Maybe I am insecure; maybe I'm doubting myself." So, I began to bring my insecurities, doubts, and fears to God in my prayers and during fasting. When you fast and pray, always lay your weaknesses before God. He won't turn you away or judge you; instead, He shines through our weaknesses. He gives us the faith, courage, strength, and power we need to overcome, as long as we come to Him with a humble heart. Praying and fasting are powerful tools for overcoming spiritual challenges. The more time you spend with God, the more victories you will achieve.

Five years ago, I found myself as a woman without direction, grappling with a shattered heart and ensnared by the temptations of the world, including alcohol, drug abuse, and promiscuity. My thoughts were clouded, and I felt utterly unproductive, struggling to rise each day. Life seemed overwhelmingly painful and dark, leaving me uncertain of my path. My sources of happiness were limited to men, friends, and alcohol, and I was unaware of my true potential, fixated instead on drinking and seeking fleeting enjoyment. In school, I struggled with math, but I cherished writing classes, as they provided an escape from reality. As I grew older, I developed a dislike for speaking English, opting to remain in bilingual classes to avoid it, and I had little interest in studying. Despite these challenges, the grace of God continued to pursue me. The unwavering love of my creator has been a constant presence in my life, with His mercy renewing each day, enabling me to share my thoughts with you through this writing.

It is through God's grace, love, and mercy that you find yourself engaging with this book today. Not only am I the author of these pages, but I also serve as the treasurer of my church—a remarkable journey for someone who once struggled with mathematics. Additionally, I have embraced the challenge of participating in the translating ministry, where I now confidently translate during services, despite my previous hesitations about speaking English. Once a month, I contribute to the children's ministry by preparing Bible studies, and I have recently embarked on a new venture by starting my own homemade fragrance business while also returning to school to pursue theology courses.

A woman who once struggled with depression, bitterness, and alcoholism transformed her life to become an author, a leader, a businesswoman, and a devoted servant of Jesus. This remarkable change occurred because she chose to follow the path that God had already laid out for her in eternity. With faith, she embraced Jesus, not knowing what awaited her on the other side. She opened her heart to Him and left behind the burdens that had held her captive. Jesus shattered her chains, liberated her, and enveloped her in His love, becoming her greatest desire. Now, she can experience joy and dream without limitations, for in Him, all things are possible. If He could do this for her, He desires to do the same for you. It is time to surrender and allow God to complete your story, as He is not finished with you yet. In the midst of uncertainty, God seeks to make you fruitful, restore you, heal you, and elevate you. Above all, He longs for a relationship with you, inviting you to know Him as the loving and merciful God who has been with you since the beginning and wishes to instill new hope in your life. Jesus has given us the Holy Spirit to guide us, and once you accept Him as your Savior, the Spirit dwells within you, assuring you that you are never alone. He serves as your comforter, friend, and guide. This journey with God may not be easy; it can be painful, challenging, and transformative, revealing deeper truths you may not have previously understood. However, I can assure you that this decision has been the most significant one I have ever made. It is a life-altering experience that brings about profound change. In Him, there is always peace, as my soul finds rest in His presence. Even in moments of fear, His words remind me that He is always by my side and that He had me in mind long before my birth. My friend, do not fear; instead, rejoice, for walking with Jesus leads to eternal life.

Points to reflect on for this chapter:

1. It is important to recognize that fear can obscure the manifestation of God's power in your life, leading to doubts about His promises and purpose.

2. When fear takes control, it hinders your ability to be productive and fruitful.

3. Embrace the opportunity to serve Jesus without fear, trusting Him to guide you toward His purpose.

4. Challenging times forge resilience and strength in individuals.

5. Stepping into the unknown can open the door to a transformative new life.

6. Your choices today can have a lasting impact, either positively or negatively, on future generations.

7. Remember, God is greater than any fear you may face.

8. You may never feel fully prepared to serve God, but by taking that initial step, He will handle the rest.

9. God has the power to transform your weaknesses into strengths.

10. The time you dedicate to your relationship with God directly correlates with the victories you will experience.

11. Surrender everything to God, He is not finished with you yet, and allow Him to craft your story.

Are you ready to embark on that initial journey into the unknown? The journey that Jesus has laid out for you in eternity. Your response will determine the testimony that awaits you!

(John 14:27 NIV)

"Peace I leave with you; my peace I give to you. I do not give to you as the world gives. Do not let your hearts be troubled, and do not be afraid."

Chapter 10

YOUR TESTIMONY

(Psalms 118:17 NLT)

"I will not die but live, and will proclaim what the LORD has done."

Chapter 10 marks a significant milestone in my writing journey. From the beginning, I approached this project with faith, and I conclude it with the same conviction. I truly believe that this book will inspire testimonies. As I write, I feel a passionate fire within me, having poured my heart into each chapter with unwavering dedication. This experience has led me to realize that perhaps this is my true calling. My deepest desire is for you to come to know Christ and to cultivate a growing relationship with the Holy Spirit. I hope that you allow God's spirit to transform and work through you. While I may not possess the power to change your narrative, I sincerely hope that my testimony ignites a spark within your spirit. If you have already accepted Jesus as your Savior, I encourage you to share the incredible works He has accomplished in your life. A testimony holds immense power; it can touch hearts, inspire reflection, prompt repentance, elevate faith, break chains, and transform lives. Your story could be the light that others desperately need. Even if your life has been challenging and your experiences have felt overwhelming, remember that your story can serve as a powerful tool for change in someone else's life. As I write this chapter, I find myself gazing out from my balcony, contemplating those who will one day read these words—YOU! I have written this for YOU! I have made myself an instrument of God's purpose, sharing my testimony in hopes of bringing deliverance and freedom to others, guiding lost souls back to the Father. No matter who you are, I urge you not to give up! What you are facing right now will not defeat you; instead, it will make you more alive and stronger in God's perfect timing. Embrace your journey, for every process, trial, and setback contributes to your testimony.

Furthermore, a testimony is a catalyst for empowerment, change, authority, growth, and transformation. The Book of Acts in the New Testament illustrates the profound impact of sharing personal experiences of what one has witnessed, the works of God, and how the Holy Spirit can embolden us to inspire transformation in others. The disciples, having spent significant time with Jesus, absorbing His teachings and witnessing miracles, were empowered by the Holy Spirit after His death and resurrection to continue the mission of spreading the Gospel. It was their moment to bear witness to the wonders they had experienced. Through the Spirit, they facilitated deliverance, healing, and miracles, driven by their willingness to share how Jesus sacrificed Himself for humanity's sins and how their lives were transformed through their relationship with him. When we engage deeply with Jesus, it ignites a desire within us to share His miracles and to serve as instruments of healing, restoration, and transformation. Today, Christianity and faith in Jesus persist because individuals continue to share the Gospel and testify about their lives changed by Christ. Will you join this mission? Will you be a vessel for God to reach others?

I encourage you, guided by the love of Christ and the teachings of Scripture, to shed your former self and embrace a life filled with love, joy, confidence, trust, and faith. While life presents its challenges, it is hope and faith that sustain us. As stated in Romans 1:17 (NIV), "The righteous will live by faith." Our faith and hope in Jesus are essential, much like the air we breathe, enabling us to navigate each day. My greatest aspiration is to stand before Jesus and hear Him proclaim, "Well done, my faithful servant." I have testified through this book that He is REAL! More real than what your eyes can see.

Jesus is indeed REAL! He has transformed my life, breaking my chains and granting me freedom. I am truly ALIVE again through Him! Jesus resides within me, and He can reside in you too if you have accepted Him as your Savior, the begotten Son of God who sacrificed Himself for our sins. So, lift your spirits! Wear a smile! As I conclude, my dear brothers and sisters in Christ, when you feel disheartened and tempted to revert to your old ways, resist that urge! Remember, we are called to live in freedom, so why indulge our flesh? Why invite death back into our lives for fleeting pleasures? The love of God and His promises are everlasting! Stay in the light, sharing your testimony with love, patience, and perseverance. Always remember your journey, the trials you faced, and the place from which God has rescued you. Do not forget the tears you shed, the pain you endured, and the effort it took to become who you are today! So why look back? While I may be in this world for now, my true home and treasures are in heaven. In the meantime, I find joy in faithfully waiting for Him, bearing witness to His goodness and mercy.

(Luke 21:13 NIV)

"And so you will bear testimony to me."

Now is your moment, my friend! Are you prepared to share the goodness of God? Become a life transformer for the kingdom of God through your testimony!

About the Author:

Tayshalee Reyes, born in Carolina, Puerto Rico, now lives in Orlando, Florida, after spending her formative years in Newark, New Jersey. A dedicated mother to her lovely daughter, Leenaysha, Tayshalee has always nurtured a deep passion for writing and storytelling. She often found herself questioning her calling, asking God, "Why do you want me to pursue something that so many others are already doing? There are so many writers out there." In her heart, she felt God's reassurance: "It's not about the quantity of writers, but the intention of the heart."

Writing has been her sanctuary during the most challenging moments of her life, providing an escape from the harsh realities she faced. Throughout her journey, she has navigated various obstacles, including being raised by a single mother, enduring bullying in school, and battling feelings of isolation and depression, which eventually led to struggles with alcohol addiction and despair. Like many, Tayshalee sought a route to happiness, but her challenges with substance abuse and mental health felt overwhelming—until she found Jesus. She is now prepared to share her story, affirming that Jesus is truly real and has the power to change lives.

Tayshalee Quotes:

"My Failures help me return stronger."

"Focus not on the magnitude of the problem,
but rather on the significant opportunity it presents."

"A journey into the unknown guides
you toward the divine purpose of God."

9 798895 971703